Surviving Greek Bureaucracy

Surviving Greek Bureaucracy

A cradle-to-grave guide to the state

ATHENS NEWS

Texts: Kathy Tzilivakis and Demetris Nellas
Telephone directory: Maria Angelopoulos
Proofreader: Dorde Crncevic
Layout: Yannis Smyrnis
Cover design: Konstantinos Georgantas
Series editor: John Psaropoulos

The chapters of this book first appeared in the Athens News, Greece's English-language weekly newspaper

ISBN 978-960-89200-4-0

Printed and bound in Athens, Greece by Psyllidis Graphic Arts
Pre-Press by Multimedia SA

Contents

Publisher's preface IX

Marriage 11, Divorce 16, Birth and Baptism 22, Child custody 27, Military service 37, Employment 44, Pensions 50, Making a will 56, Rights and obligations of EU citizens 65, Rights and obligations of non-EU citizens 69, Greek citizenship 86, Voting rights 89, Greek passports 90, Foreign driving permits 92, Greek driving permits 93, Renting a home 95, Buying a home 97, Greek language certificate 103, Translating official documents 105, The Greek tax roll number (AFM) 107, The Citizens' Service Centre (KEP) 108, The ombudsman 109, The EU ombudsman 111, The banking ombudsman 113, Solvit: the EU trouble-shooter 115, Consumer rights 118, Transporting a dead body overseas 121, Filling in tax forms 123

Telephone directory: Utilities 163, Airports 164, Public services 165, Citizens' rights 166, Government 168, Embassies 170, Community organisations 184, Foreign institutes and schools 196, Miscellaneous organisations 202, Places of worship 203, Athletic organisations 208, Hospitals 210, Transport 219, Museums and sites 220, Theatres and halls 226, Attica municipalities 226

Publisher's preface

Surviving Greek Bureaucracy has been designed to guide you through your interactions with the public sector. Those interactions are inevitable if you decide to live here, work, pay taxes, get married, have children and bequeath your estate to them.

Such mundane information may seem as though it ought to be ubiquitous, but in fact it is not. Although more and more government is moving onto the web, Greek bureaucracy still operates largely by word of mouth. That is especially hard on non-native populations, repatriated Greeks and foreign-educated Greeks, most of whom are used to functional bureaucracies.

These are the communities we have set out to serve in Greece's weekly, English-language newspaper, the *Athens News*. Over the years we have explained such things as who is liable for army service and how to file taxes. Now we have collated this expertise.

We hope that this book will make Greece more navigable. We also invite you to improve future editions by writing in with your comments for improvements and additions at *atheditor@dolnet.gr*.

John Psaropoulos
Editor
Athens News

ATHENS NEWS

Marriage

What's a Thursday night *krevati*? Why aren't the bride and groom allowed to say anything during their wedding? Whether you're going to be in one or attend one, a Greek Orthodox wedding is chock-full of traditions you might not know.

From the throwing of a baby boy onto the marital bed to the eating of the sweet *koufeta* after the rice has been thrown, here are the ABCs of a traditional Greek wedding.

Before the wedding

After months of planning, all is set to go. The invitations have been mailed or personally delivered to the guests. The reception menu and wine list have been double-checked. The bride's gown and the groom's suit are proudly hanging in the closet. It's time for the *krevati* - the blessing of the marital bed - and a chance for the couple to show their new home (*spitiko*) to friends and family.

The *krevati* is a tradition practised across the country. It's a party held on the Thursday night before the wedding (which is usually on a Saturday or Sunday). According to this Greek custom, the bride makes the bed together with girls and unmarried women. The guests then proceed, one by one, to throw money onto the couple's bed in hopes that their union will be fruitful and prosperous. A baby boy is also thrown onto the bed as a symbol of fertility.

The church service

The Greek Orthodox ceremony is full of symbolism and quite different from weddings in Western Europe and the United States or Canada.

One distinction is that the bride and groom in Greece do not exchange vows. There are no "I dos".

Also, the bride does not walk down the aisle to meet the groom at the altar. The groom waits for the bride outside the church. The bride usually arrives in a car or horse-drawn carriage, but not before she circles the church several times to the applauding of the guests.

Finally, the groom and the bride meet. According to tradition, the groom kisses the hand of the father of the bride. He then hands a bouquet of flowers to the bride and the two walk into the church and down to the altar together.

The guests follow the bride and groom. Inside the church, there is no separation of the guests of the bride and groom. People sit wherever they would like. Most opt to stand as close as possible to the altar so as not to miss the ceremony. The atmosphere in the church is casual, as guests converse freely with one another throughout the ceremony.

At the altar, the bride stands on the left and the groom on the right. The parents, siblings and the *koumbaroi* (the marriage sponsors who are like the best man and maid of honour) join the couple.

The service begins. The wedding rings are blessed by the priest. With the rings in his right hand, the priest makes the sign of the cross over the heads of the bride and groom. He then places them on the third fingers of their right hands.

Now it's the *koumbaros'* turn. He takes the rings and swaps them three times (symbolising Holy Trinity) between the bride and groom's finger.

The hands of the bride and groom are then joined by the priest to symbolise their union. They are not allowed to separate until after the ceremony.

Near the end of the ceremony, the priest blesses the *stefana* (two crowns joined by a ribbon). The *koumbaros* crosses them over the bride and groom's head three times before placing them on their head.

Reading from the Gospel of John (the passage where Jesus turns water into wine, the first "miracle"), the priest pours wine into a glass for the bride and groom to drink. They take three sips each.

Probably the most exciting part of the ceremony (especially for the guests) is the traditional walk around the altar. United by the *stefana*, the bride and groom circle the altar three times as guests shower them with rice to wish them much happiness.

The ceremony ends. The priest blesses the couple and takes off their *stefana*. He then uses the Bible to separate their hands, signifying that only God can dissolve their marriage.

The signing of the registrar signals the end of the wedding ceremony. The bride and groom are required to sign it to make the marriage legal. Two witnesses are required. It's usually the *koumbaros* and the *koumbara* (bridesmaid).

The receiving line

The receiving line is usually formed right after the ceremony at the church. This is a chance for the bride and groom, their parents and the *koumbaros* and *koumbara* to thank the guests and for the guests to wish the newlyweds a happy life together. Traditionally, guests are supposed to say *Na zisete* (literally, "may you live", but meaning "may you live long and happily") to the happy couple, *Panta axy-ee* ("may you be worthy of performing this honour for other couples") to the *koumbaros* and *koumbara* and *Na zisoune* ("may they live long and happily") to the proud parents. In return, the bride and groom thank their guests and wish those who are single *Kai sta dika sas* ("and to your future wedding").

The bomboniere

These are the gifts (special keepsakes) for the guests - a tradition that can be traced back hundreds of years. The *bomboniere* always includes *koufeta* - sugar-coated almonds - wrapped in tulle.

How to get hitched

Under Greek law, Greeks and foreign nationals may be married in either civil or religious ceremonies. While there is no residence requirement for foreigners wishing to marry in Greece, they should be in possession of a residence permit or a tourist visa. This does not apply to EU nationals.

Civil marriages

Couples wishing to marry must submit (in person) the documents listed below to their local municipality (*dimarhio*) or to the president of their community (*proedros kinotitas*) to apply for a marriage licence. Marriage licences are issued seven days after the application is submitted and are valid for six months. Civil ceremonies may be performed anywhere in Greece.

The couple must submit another application to the mayor or the president of the community in which they wish to be married. This official then sets the wedding date. Two witnesses, provided by the couple, must attend the wedding ceremony. One of the witnesses may act as an interpreter. Witnesses must present official identification cards or passports.

Religious marriages

The documents listed below must be submitted to the priest who is to perform the ceremony. Foreigners also need to submit an official translation of their baptism certificate or another document showing they are of Orthodox Christian faith. If they are not, they will have to be baptised into the Orthodox Church. The priest will apply for and obtain the marriage licences.

The documents required for the marriage licence
▶ A Greek ID card or a valid passport or other travel document
▶ Certified photocopy of both the bride's and groom's birth certificate with an official translation from the Greek foreign

ministry (if it is not in Greek)

▶ If applicable, a document verifying the termination of a previous marriage (death certificate or final divorce papers) with an official translation (if it's not in Greek).

▶ Confirmation by the foreigner's consulate in Greece that there is no impediment to the marriage; for instance, that there is no existing marriage and that neither party is under 18 years old

▶ The wedding must be announced in a Greek daily, and a copy of the announcement must be submitted. It should be in Greek with names written in Greek characters. This is not necessary in small towns.

▶ There is also a fee of 15 euros.

Registration of a marriage

All marriages, civil and religious, must be registered at the local vital statistics office *(lixiarhio)* within 40 days of the ceremony.

Divorce

Nikos and Sheila live in Thessaloniki. Nikos is a public school teacher. Sheila owns a travel agency. They marry. Sheila's business skyrockets. Nikos is very enthusiastic and supportive of Sheila's business and also takes care of the daily household chores so that she can focus on her business. Sheila expands her business and opens a branch in London, her home town.

What if Nikos and Sheila decide to divorce? If the divorce case is heard in Greece, Nikos stands to gain a portion of Sheila's fortune because he provided the circumstances that allowed her to focus on the business. If they file for divorce in England, he does not.

Divorce is never easy, but it's even harder if the separating spouses have different nationalities and do not know where they should, or can, file for divorce. According to European Union law (Brussels II/Rome II Regulation, 2201/2003), couples may apply for a divorce in the member state of their habitual residence or in the member state of their nationality.

Legislation significantly varies between the member states. Swedish law, for instance, does not require any ground for divorce. In Greece, Slovakia, Ireland, the Netherlands and the United Kingdom, irreparable breakdown of the marriage is the only grounds for divorce.

The annulment of a marriage is prohibited in Sweden and Finland. Legislation in Malta does not even allow for divorce.

The European Commission - the EU's executive arm - is currently seeking a way to help "international couples" to dissolve their marriage without the additional problems of trying to figure out which country they should file for divorce in. There are currently no EU-wide provisions on applicable law in divorce. The Brussels II/Rome II regulation includes rules on jurisdiction and recognition in matrimonial matters, but does not comprise rules on applicable law.

A new European Council regulation (to be known as Rome III) was published in July 2006 and is expected to come into force in March 2008. It will enable couples to choose which EU country deals with their divorce proceedings and which law governs the action.

"The increasing mobility of citizens within the European Union has resulted in an increasing number of international marriages where the spouses are of different nationalities, or live in different member states or live in a member state of which they are not nationals," says the European Commission in its Green Paper (proposal for the new regulation). "In the event that an international couple decide to divorce, several laws may be invoked. The aim of the rules on applicable law, often referred to as 'conflict-of-law rules', is to determine which of the different laws will apply. In view of the high number of divorces within the European Union, applicable law and international jurisdiction in divorce matters affect a considerable number of citizens."

Greek law

Landmark legislation (law 1329) passed by the Greek parliament in 1983 established two types of divorce. The first is in the case that both spouses consent to the divorce and the second when the marital relationship has undergone irreparable damage. A couple may also lawfully divorce after four years of separation.

In the first scenario the marriage should have lasted at least one year and the couple must agree on the custody of their children. In the second scenario the couple must go to court and convince a judge that they cannot reconcile their differences to save their marriage. The court decides on the custody of their children.

Before 1983, a divorce could only be filed by the so-called blameless spouse. The grounds for divorce were limited to adultery, bigamy, miserable living conditions, abandonment of more than two years, a serious disruption to the marital relationship, insanity which lasted for at least four years, leprosy and impotence that has lasted for at least three years and continues to the day the divorce papers are filed.

As for alimony, the 1983 law states that both spouses have the right to demand alimony regardless of who is to blame for the breakup. Alimony, however, is only paid out to the spouse who is caring for the children and cannot work, to the spouse who cannot support himself/herself and to the spouse who is continuing his/her education (for up to three years).

The ex-spouse is no longer entitled to alimony if he/she remarries or cohabits with someone out of wedlock but as husband and wife.

Before 1983, alimony was paid by the husband to the wife only if he was at fault for divorce and she did not have her own source of income. However, the wife would be denied alimony if she was to blame for the divorce. She would also have to pay alimony to her ex-husband if he was physically or mentally incapable of supporting himself.

Divorce by consent
▶ After one year of marriage
▶ Both spouses agree on issues concerning alimony (spousal support), property division, child custody/visitation rights and child support. They make a joint petition to the court
▶ No litigation
Contested divorce:
▶ No agreement
▶ One spouse files for divorce
▶ Litigation, including trial before a family court judge
Grounds for divorce:
▶ Breakdown of the marital relationship caused by one or both spouses
▶ Presumption of breakdown, such as in cases where one

spouse is accused of bigamy, adultery or desertion
▶ At least four years of separation
▶ If one spouse is presumed missing or dead
Legal consequences of divorce:
▶ No obligation to live together as man and wife
▶ No obligation to take decisions jointly
Division of property:
Joint ownership ends upon the termination of a marriage contract. Each spouse receives what he/she is entitled to under the rules of joint ownership and the distribution of common property.

Each spouse is entitled to property that belongs to him/her even if it has been used by both spouses. This can be property that each spouse had before the marriage or acquired during the marriage by gift or inheritance.

The equitable distribution of property can become one of the most contentious issues in a divorce.

Child custody The court may grant sole custody to one of the parents or joint custody to both. It may grant custody to a third party.

Alimony (spousal support) The court may decide that one spouse must provide the lower-income spouse with money for living expenses (in addition to the money provided by child support). By law, the marriage should have lasted for at least one year.

Alimony may be paid to the ex-spouse on a monthly basis or as a lump sum payment.

Legal separation: In practice, separation means that although a couple are not divorced, they are not living as husband and wife. Under law it is grounds for divorce.

Annulment The court rules that the marriage never existed from the beginning. A marriage may be annulled in the following cases as specified by Greek law:

❱ Marriage contracted by parties under the age of 18
❱ Marriage between blood relations or between adoptive parent and adopted child
❱ Marriage contracted if either of the parties was not of sound mind or if the consent of either spouse was obtained by violence or the threat of violence
❱ If at the time of the marriage one of the parties was already bound by a previous marriage
❱ If the consent of either of the parties is obtained by fraud

Divorce around Europe

❱ Irreparable breakdown of the marriage is the only grounds for divorce in Greece, Germany, Slovakia, Ireland, the Netherlands and the United Kingdom. In Belgium, irretrievable breakdown underlies all types of divorce, but is not in itself grounds for divorce. Irreparable breakdown normally has to be supported by proof. Proof may include a period of separation (France, Spain, Italy, Germany, the United Kingdom, Austria, Latvia), minimal age of the spouses (Belgium, Luxembourg), a minimal duration of the marriage (Greece, Belgium), statement of the reasons (Austria, the Netherlands) or a written agreement between the spouses on the exercise of parental responsibility and property relations between the spouses (Belgium, Greece, Italy, France, Austria, Luxembourg, Portugal, the Netherlands). Polish law requires the court to verify that the breakdown of the marriage is not only irreparable but also complete. In some member states, mutual consent makes it unnecessary to investigate the reasons for the breakdown (the Czech Republic, Hungary).
❱ Some member states (Belgium, France, Luxembourg, Austria, Portugal, Denmark, Cyprus and Lithuania) provide "fault-based" divorce. This requires serious or renewed violations of marital duties and obligations, rendering it intolerable for the spouses to continue living together. This covers, for example, domestic

violence, failure to fulfil financial obligations and adultery. Certain jurisdictions that do not provide for fault-based divorce nevertheless take into account grounds such as adultery, unreasonable behaviour and desertion as presumptions to establish the irreparable breakdown of the marriage.

❭ Factual separation constitutes autonomous grounds for divorce in certain member states (Belgium, France, Denmark, Ireland, Luxembourg, Portugal, Spain, Cyprus, Latvia and Lithuania). The duration of the factual separation varies (from six months in Denmark to five years in Cyprus). In Ireland, it is only one of several cumulative conditions.

❭ Sweden and Finland do not require any ground for divorce, but merely a consideration period of six months. The consideration period is always required under Finnish law, whereas Swedish law only requires it if one of the spouses does not consent or if the spouses have custody of a child under 16 years of age. Conversely, no consideration period is required if the divorce application is based on consent and the spouses do not have custody of children below the age of 16.

❭ All member states, with the exception of Sweden and Finland, provide for marriage annulment.

Birth and Baptism

Naming a baby is no mean feat, but choosing a name may be easier in Greece than in other countries where parents spend months consulting books and internet websites trying to find the perfect one. Here, children are named after their grandparents. It's tradition and it's expected.

The first boy and first girl are customarily named after their paternal grandparents, the second of each gender after the maternal grandparents. So, if a couple had two boys and two girls, it would not be until the fifth child that they could pick a name. But even then it should be a saint's name if the baby is to be baptised.

The baptism ceremony

In the Greek Orthodox Church, the baptism begins with an exorcism at the entrance of the church. The priest calls on the godparent (the baby's spiritual sponsor) to renounce the devil three times on behalf of the child.

The baby is then undressed and the priest immerses him/her three times into the font *(kolymbithra)* filled with blessed water. The priest repeats: "The servant of God *(name)* is baptised in the name of the Father and of the Son and of the Holy Spirit."

The priest then takes the consecrated oil and anoints the baby with the sign of the cross on the forehead, eyes, nose, mouth and ears.

In the Orthodox Church, the baptism concludes with the sacrament of confirmation, or *Chrismation*. It literally means "an anointing" from the Ancient Greek word *chrizo*. The baby is then dressed in a new set of clothes symbolising its rebirth - traditionally white, the colour of purity. Then the priest, together with the godparent(s) and the baby, circles the font three times.

The priest cuts four locks of hair from the child's head in the form of a cross. This is an expression of gratitude. Hair is a symbol of strength in the Old Testament.

Immediately following the baptism, the baby becomes a full member of the Orthodox Church. The lighting of a white candle symbolises the Christian faith of the baby. The entire ceremony lasts about 45 minutes.

Dogma versus tradition

Must the parents have their marriage recognised by the Orthodox Church?

Not according to dogma. In theory, the parents can be of different denominations, different faiths or unmarried. What matters most to the church is the induction of a new member, the child. A chauvinistic tradition, however, has come to demand that the parents must be Orthodox and often requires a conversion before the baptism. Some stubborn priests even refuse to recognise civil marriage. One enterprising father was forced to adopt his son in order to baptise him, because the church did not recognise the father's civil marriage to the mother.

Do the godparents have to be Orthodox?

Yes (though not necessarily Greek Orthodox) because they confess the faith on behalf of the child (*omologia*).

Can they convert on the spot?

Yes, the non-Orthodox godparent must agree to be baptised first. If there are many godparents, it is the principal, or *anadohos*, who must be Orthodox. He or she is the godparent who receives the child from the font.

Can the civil name and baptism name differ?

In theory, yes. It is not church dogma to baptise only with saints' names, although a priest has a duty to try and persuade the parents to choose a Christian name. In practice, though, tradition is stricter than dogma and most priests now demand that the parents choose a saint's name. However, the name the child is registered under with the municipal authorities is the legally binding name.

Does the ceremony have to take place in an Orthodox church?

In theory, the ceremony can take place in any consecrated church (diaspora Greeks routinely use other churches, particularly Anglican, Lutheran and Reformed). In fact, the ceremony need not take place in a church at all. Jesus was baptised in the river Jordan, and early Christian baptisms were often done in rivers or the sea.

Can an Orthodox ceremony be done in English instead of Greek?

Yes. Or French. Or any language.

Can Orthodoxy do multiple baptism?

Yes. The water is blessed once, and any number of people can then be baptised in it. The Greek Orthodox Church often does such mass baptisms in Africa.

Paperwork and money

The paper trail begins as soon as we are born. The parents must register the birth at the municipality in which the baby was born.

All that is needed is a photocopy of their Greek ID card or passport or residence permit. Hospitals have an in-house birth registry that issues the parents with a *proto*-certificate. Private hospitals will also send directly to the local municipality a document signed by the doctor who performed the delivery, stating the child's gender, weight and date of birth. Public hospitals give this document to the parents. This registration is free if it is done within 10 days. If not, it costs 4.40 euros, and 13.50 euros if it is done after three months.

When the parents decide on the child's first name they declare this to the vital statistics office (*lyxiarheio*) of the municipality where the child was born. This requires the presence of both parents. Greek citizens are required to show their ID card, passport or driver's licence. Non-Greek citizens are required to show their passport or residence permit. If one parent cannot make it to the *lyxiarheio*, he/she must sign a proxy consent form certified by the police or at a Citizens' Service Centre (KEP). If the absent parent is outside the country, the proxy must be signed at the local Greek consulate. The municipality issues the final birth certificate with the child's full name.

Church and state

To baptise the child, the church requires either the birth registration or the final birth certificate. A few days after the baptism, the church will issue a baptism certificate, which the child will need if it is ever to be married in an Orthodox ceremony, or to become a godparent in the Orthodox Church.

After the ceremony, parents or guardians may also register the baptism with their local *lyxiarheio*, although this is not required by law. All that is required is the certificate signed by the priest who conducted the baptism and the Greek ID card or other form of ID of one of the parents or guardians.

If the baptism is registered within 90 days, there is no charge. If it is registered after the 90-day period, the procedure costs 4.40 euros. If the baptism is registered five or more months later, the procedure costs 13.50 euros.

Parents *must* register the baby's name at the *lyxiarheio* either before or after the baptism. The baptism is merely a ceremony, not a legal act.

Godparent survival kit

For the ceremony

You have to purchase the complete set of new clothes the child will wear, including shoes and a hat. Some ultra-traditional households also insist on silk breeches. You bring the olive oil with which the child will be anointed and the gargantuan white candle that will be lit once, for five minutes, at the end of the ceremony.

Most importantly, you bring the gold cross the child wears throughout his or her life. Some godparents also give silver or gold identity bracelets.

You must articulate certain responses to the priest, and even though most priests will guide you through the ceremony, it is just as well to purchase a copy of the liturgy beforehand and rehearse (the slim volume retails for a few euros, but is often available free from the church).

Finally, godparents often provide the cross lapel pins given out to congregants.

Officially, baptisms are free. Church priests should not charge a fee to perform the ritual. However, some do request a "donation" (sometimes as high as several hundred euros) from the godparents.

After the ceremony

In the Christian Church, godparents have a duty to make sure that the child is raised in the Christian faith. More generally, they are mentors and considered close family friends who take a special interest in the child.

One of their first duties is to make sure the child receives its first communion 40 days after baptism. They have to show up at the child's birthdays and namedays with presents, and give the child an Easter *lambada* (candle) - along with a toy. It goes without saying that they have to give the child a Christmas present.

Child custody

Can parents kidnap their own children? Yes, and it's not such a rare phenomenon, especially since divorce rates and international custody disputes are on the rise.

According to the justice ministry, most of the international child abduction cases tried in Greece involve Greeks married to Australians, Germans, Swedes, Britons and Americans.

"Many cases of international child abduction by parents began when the child, upon the approval of both parents, travelled abroad, but subsequently was not allowed to return to the country of his/her habitual residence," says the justice ministry in a report published on its website. "Sometimes, even if there are no problems in a marriage, when the foreign parent returns to his/her country of origin, the latter [may decide]... not to return. This is not a rare phenomenon, since the behaviour of a person may change when he/she returns to the place, where he/she grew up."

Under Greek law, parental responsibility is shared between both parents, provided they are married and live together.

If the parents divorce, they may decide between themselves or go to court over who will have parental custody of their child. The court may grant responsibility to one or both the parents, divide it between them or grant it to someone else.

In March 2005, the European Union enacted new legislation (EC 2201/2003), intended to deter parental child abduction between member states. The regulation prevails over national legislation and applies to all decisions on parental responsibility and to extrajudicial (out-of-court) agreements.

According to European Commission Vice-President Franco Frattini, the regulation is a "milestone in the creation of a common judicial area in family matters and a significant step forward in the EU policy to protect and promote the rights of the child".

"The new rules on child abduction will ensure the prompt return of abducted children to their member states of origin," says Frattini. "The regulation will also reinforce the fundamental right of the child to maintain regular contacts with both parents by allowing judgements on visiting rights to circulate freely between member states."

According to the regulation, the courts of the member state where the child was "habitually resident" before the abduction are competent to decide on the custody. The regulation also stresses the right of the child to be heard, unless the judge deems it inappropriate owing to the child's age and degree of maturity.

It is also worth noting that under the 1980 Hague Convention on International Child Abduction (Greece is a signatory) courts have the right to send back children to the countries where they are "habitually resident".

This means that if a child born in Canada is illegally brought to Greece by his/her Greek parent, the court must send the child back to Canada.

Greek law

Child abduction by a parent is a criminal offence in Greece. Article 324 of the Greek Criminal Code explicitly states that a parent who abducts his/her child is subject to a maximum of three years in prison.

When one parent's custody rights have been violated by the other's "wrongful removal or retention" of the child, that parent may request the return of the child based on the Hague Convention. There are two ways to do this: One is by applying to the Greek justice ministry (application forms are available online *www.ministryofjustice.gr*). The other involves hiring a lawyer and taking the case to court in Greece.

Note: the application to the justice ministry and all attached documentation must be translated into Greek. After reviewing the application, the ministry forwards it to the public prosecutor. The non-custodial parent is then notified and negotiations are arranged for the child's return. If the child is not returned voluntarily, the public prosecutor will file an application with the Greek court.

The Hague Convention requires that abduction cases be expedited.

The ministry also lists the following three "preventive steps".

▶ Keep a record of addresses and telephone numbers of relatives and friends of the other parent

▶ Keep a record of important information about the other parent, including passport number, driving licence number and vehicle registration number

▶ Keep recent photographs of your child

In cases of international abductions, the justice ministry can help parents in Greece file an application to foreign authorities for the return of the child. The ministry can also assist parents to locate the child in another country.

What the ministry cannot do is to intervene in divorce cases. It cannot pay court or other expenses and it cannot act as a lawyer or represent parents in court.

The ministry's website also stresses that while the Hague Convention is a very useful legal tool for the return of an abducted child, the parents should try to work things out. "Sometimes, friends and relatives can help you reach a compromise and limit tension and thus achieve the return of your child easier," says the ministry. "Compromise and conciliation are often the most realistic and painless solution for all."

'Not fully compliant'

According to the United States Department of State's 2006 Report on Compliance with the Hague Convention on the Civil Aspects of International Child Abduction, Greece is a country that is "not fully compliant".

"While the Greek central authority [the justice ministry]

processes convention applications in a satisfactory manner, court hearings are seriously delayed," says the report. "Of particular concern is the inordinately long period of time that elapses between a hearing and notification of the court's decision... [Also] the courts exhibit a nationalistic bias in favour of Greek parents and take into account other inappropriate considerations of the home environment such as the alleged benefits of the child living surrounded by his or her extended Greek family."

The report also notes that the Greek courts "frequently accept parents' claims that the left-behind parent was abusive or generally unfit to be a parent without clear evidence in support of these assertions". And that the Greek courts "do not fully investigate these claims".

Cases in point

In 1996, the Court of First Instance in Thessaloniki awarded the mother, a resident of Alaska, custody of her two children, aged 7 and 9. The father, a Greek citizen, was granted visitation rights.

The facts of the case involve a Greek father, who had brought the two children to Greece in 1994 without the required authorisation from their mother. The mother filed an application on "wrongful removal and retention" through the Greek justice ministry. The children were eventually reunited with their mother in Alaska.

One case that made it all the way to the Supreme Court (*Areios Pagos*) involved a Greek father and a Swedish mother and their two children (a boy and a girl).

The Supreme Court cancelled a decision of the Greek Court of Appeals on the grounds of insufficient standard of proof, as required by the Hague Convention. The Thessaloniki Court of Appeals had ordered that the boy stay in Greece with his father after reasoning that his return to Sweden would endanger his physical and mental wellbeing. The court had also ordered that the girl be returned to her mother in Sweden.

Another case, which was heard on appeal and decided by the New York Court of Appeals, is exceptionally complex because of conflicting custody awards issued by the courts of Greece and New York. The case involved the father, an American citizen, the mother, a Greek citizen, and two children, dual citizens of the United States and Greece.

During a family vacation in Greece in 1995, the parents separated. The father returned to the United States, while the mother remained in Greece with the children. In 1995, a Greek court awarded the mother temporary custody of the children. Soon after, the father filed for divorce and child custody in New York. He was awarded temporary custody in July 1997 and permanent custody in November 1997.

The father filed a petition with the Greek justice ministry requesting that the children be returned to New York. He took the case to Greece's Supreme Court, which ruled in favour of the mother. The mother was granted primary custody of the children. The father won visitation rights.

In October 2000, the father took the children to the United States without the mother's consent. The mother filed an International Child Abduction Remedies Act (ICARA) proceeding, requesting the return of the two children to Greece. The issue under consideration was to decide whether Greece or the United States was the habitual residence of the children. According to the Greek court, the children's habitual residence was Greece since they were there from 1995 to 2000.

The Greek Supreme Court ordered that the children be returned to their mother in Greece.

In 2001, the New York Court of Appeals accepted the facts as applied by the Greek Supreme Court.

The Hague Convention: The Hague Convention on the Civil

Aspects of International Child Abduction is an intergovernmental agreement reached at The Hague on 25 October 1980. It entered into force on 1 December 1983 and governs issues related to parental kidnapping or the removal of children under the age of 16 across international borders involving the jurisdiction of different countries' courts.

The objective of the convention is to secure the prompt return of children wrongfully removed to, or retained in, any contracting state and to ensure that the rights of custody and of access under the law of one contracting state are effectively respected in the other contracting states.

More than 80 countries have ratified the convention. Countries that have not done so are mainly located in the Middle East, Africa, Asia and Central Asia.

While Greece was one of the first four countries to sign the convention on 25 October 1980, it waited 12 years before ratifying it.

Questions and answers

Who has the parental responsibility for a child?

As a general rule, the child's parents have parental responsibility, provided they are married and live together. If either of them dies; is declared missing, presumed dead; or is deprived of the parental responsibility, parental responsibility is exercised solely by the other parent. In the same way, if the court decides that there are other valid reasons why one parent is unable to exercise parental responsibility, or if one parent has no capacity to enter into legal transactions or has only limited capacity to do so, parental responsibility is exercised by the other parent.

In the case of an adopted child, parental responsibility is exercised by the adoptive parents. If a child is born out of wedlock, parental responsibility is exercised by the mother.

If the parents divorce, how is the question of parental

responsibility determined?

In a divorce by consent, the parents agree on the way they propose to exercise parental responsibility or custody over the child, and attach it to the application for the dissolution of their marriage which they submit to the single-judge court (*monomeles*) of first instance. The procedure followed is that for non-contentious cases.

If instead they apply to the multi-member court (*polymeles*) of first instance on grounds of irretrievable breakdown, the procedure followed is that for marital disputes. They may make a request that parental responsibility be granted to one of the two, or to both, or they may bring separate proceedings before the single-judge court of first instance according to article 681B of the Civil Code. The judge will decide based on what is in the child's best interest. If imminent danger or urgency arises in connection with a divorce or separation, the single-judge court of first instance may grant an injunction determining the issue of parental responsibility on a temporary basis.

What if the parents agree on who will have custody of their children?

They submit a written agreement before the court. The court considers whether the agreement is in the child's best interest. In case of a divorce by consent, submission of such agreement is obligatory when underage children are involved.

If the parents cannot agree, what are the alternative means for solving the conflict without going to court?

There are none.

If the parents go to court, what issues will the judge take into consideration?

The judge will take into consideration each parent's financial and social status, as well as who will provide the best environment for the child's physical and mental upbringing; also, the child's bond with each parent and siblings. Depending on the child's age and maturity, the court may take into consideration the child's own opinion.

To which court or authority should I turn if I want to lodge an application on parental responsibility? Which formalities must be respected and which documents shall I attach to my application?
The court with jurisdiction in cases of parental responsibility is generally the single-judge court (*monomeles*) of first instance. However, if the application for parental responsibility is included in an application for divorce on grounds of irretrievable breakdown or an application for an annulment of the marriage, the appropriate court is the multi-member court (*polymeles*) of first instance.

In the case of citizens of other European Union member states, the court with territorial jurisdiction is the court of the country specified by articles 2 and 3 of EU Council Regulation (EC) No 1347/2000 - in the "place of the last joint residence of the married couple" or the one in the place of residence of the defendant. The application is lodged with the secretariat of the court, the trial date is set and the applicant's lawyer sees to it that a copy is served to the defendant. If it is to be served in Greece, the copy is served by a bailiff. If it is to be served abroad, a copy of the application is given to the appropriate public prosecutor, who in turn sends it to the ministry of foreign affairs in order for it to be served to the defendant according to the laws of the foreign country.

Also, a copy of the petition is served to the prosecutor and a summary is published in two newspapers, one of which is published in Athens and the other in the district of the court where the case is to be tried.

For the trial, written statements are lodged setting out the claims of the two parties and their documentary evidence, and witnesses are examined in order to prove the allegations of each side.

A "social investigation" by the social services is conducted before the date of the trial and a detailed report is submitted to the court. If the court deems it necessary, it will also hear the child's opinion.

After some time the court delivers its judgement, deciding how parental responsibility is to be exercised.

Is an emergency procedure available?

Yes. When there is urgency or imminent danger, provisional and precautionary measures may be sought from the single-judge court (*monomeles*) of first instance. An immediate trial date is set and the court ruling is usually delivered sooner. Otherwise, the procedure followed is based on article 681B of the Code of Civil Procedure.

Is it possible to appeal against a decision on parental responsibility?

Yes.

What should I do to have a decision on parental responsibility that is issued by a court in another EU member state recognised and enforced in Greece? Which procedure applies in these cases?

According to Council Regulation (EC) 1347/2000, judgements delivered in an EU member state are automatically recognised across the bloc. A person who wants to have a judgement on parental responsibility recognised in Greece must submit an application to the single-judge court of first instance. Along with the application, the following documents must also be submitted:

▶ A copy of the judgement
▶ A certificate stating the court which delivered the judgement, the persons concerned, whether the judgement was given in default of appearance and that the judgement is final and not subject to appeal, whether legal aid was granted etc
▶ A certificate from the court of first instance stating that no other judgement has been issued to date between the same parties regarding the same case

After receiving a trial date, the applicant must serve a copy of the application to the defendant, along with the document setting the trial date and a summons to appear at the hearing. The Greek court may not review the jurisdiction of the court of the EU member state that delivered the judgement. The Greek court considers whether recognising the decision would be contrary to its own policy.

To which court should I turn in Greece to oppose the recognition of a decision on parental responsibility issued by a court in another member state? Which procedure applies in these cases?

The case should be brought before the court of appeal. The deadline for appeal is one month after passing the judgement, or two months from passing the judgement if the party against whom recognition is sought is normally resident in a member state other than that in which enforcement was ordered.

The judgement of the court of appeal can be challenged at the Greek Supreme Court.

Which is the applicable law in a proceeding on parental responsibility where the child or the parties do not live in Greece or are of different nationalities?

The law applicable to parental responsibility is as follows, in order:

1. the law of the last common nationality of parents and children
2. the law of their last joint normal residence
3. the law of the child's nationality; if the child is of Greek and foreign nationality, then the law of the Greek nationality applies. If the child has multiple foreign nationalities, then the law that applies is the one of the nationality to which the child has the strongest links

▶ The *Athens News* consulted the European Judicial Network in Civil and Commercial Matters and the John Tripidakis Law Offices in Glyfada (*www.greeklawyersonline.net*)

Military service

For men only! Military service in Greece is obligatory for all fit and able-bodied Greek men between the ages of 18 and 45.

The ministry of defence tries to keep track of all boys born in Greece and abroad to at least one Greek parent. This list is based on registries kept by municipalities nationwide and by Greek consulates around the world.

Note: All individuals whose mother or father holds Greek citizenship is entitled to acquire Greek citizenship automatically (without the process of naturalisation). Before 1984, only children born to a Greek father could automatically acquire Greek citizenship.

The Greek government had promised that the mandatory military service would be reduced by 2008 or even abolished completely. Too few volunteers for the professional military, however, have forced the government to reconsider.

Most Greek parents, however, want their sons to serve in the military. Conscription serves as a rite of passage. The first haircut at boot camp (basic training) marks the start of turning a boy into a man.

Your questions answered

The following answers are based on Greek laws and information published by the defence ministry and Greek consulates abroad, as well as telephone interviews with officials at local conscription offices.

Do I have to serve?

All fit and able-bodied men who have Greek citizenship must serve. The Greek constitution (article 4, paragraph 6) explicitly states that "every Greek citizen (men only) who is capable of carrying a weapon is obliged to contribute to the defence of the country as stipulated by law".

According to law 3421/2005 (passed by the parliament in November 2005), Greek men are obliged to serve in the country's armed forces. Mandatory service also applies to the son of a Greek citizen who was born and/or raised abroad.

Greek men registered as "permanent resident abroad" or "immigrant" and do not wish to reside permanently in Greece, however, are exempt from mandatory military service. They may lose this special status (and be obliged to serve in the military) if they stay in Greece for more than six months at any given time between the ages of 10 and 45.

According to the law, permanent residents abroad (*monimoi katioikoi exoterikou*) are those who have a Greek parent and who were born abroad. They must also have resided abroad permanently and continuously (for more than 180 days per calendar year) until their 18th birthday. Their parents should have also resided permanently abroad between their son's 10th and 18th birthday.

Note: Greek boys studying in Greece while their parents remain permanent residents abroad will not lose their status of permanent resident abroad. They may stay in Greece for up to 12 years (consecutively or at intervals). Proof of studies at officially recognised schools or universities in Greece is necessary.

For the purposes of conscription, the status of immigrant (*metanasti*) applies to all males who have a Greek parent and who were born in Greece but who emigrated to another country (with the exception of European Union countries and Egypt, Algeria, the United Arab Emirates, Iran, Jordan, Israel, Kuwait, Lebanon, Libya, Morocco, Muscat and Oman, Saudi Arabia, Syria, Turkey, Tunisia, Yemen and countries of the former Soviet Union) after the age of 10. This status also includes men who were born abroad and moved to Greece after the age of 10.

Those with the immigrant status may visit Greece for up to 180 days (six months) per calendar year up to the age 45 without being required to serve in the military.

How long is the mandatory service?

The duration of service in all three branches of the military (army, navy and airforce) is 12 months for Greek males born and raised in Greece.

Those who have the status of *permanent resident abroad* or *immigrant*, however, are only required to serve six months (usually in the army). They also have the choice of serving two months every year for three years. If they are 35 years of age or older, they may serve 45 days and buy out the remaining four-and-a-half months of service. This costs 3,645 euros.

Some Greek men born and raised in Greece are also entitled to a reduced six-month-duration military service. For instance, scientists conducting research are only required to serve between three and six months. They are, however, obliged to buy off the remaining duration at about 300 euros per month.

Also eligible for a reduced six-month service:
▶ The oldest brother in a family with six children
▶ The only or eldest son in a family where both parents are incapable of employment or are deceased
▶ Fathers of two or more children
▶ Married men whose spouse is incapable of working
▶ Naturalised Greek citizens
▶ Men who have served at least six months in the armed forces in another European Union member state

Eligible for nine-month service:
▶ The two oldest brothers in a family of four siblings
▶ The only or eldest son in a family where one parent is incapable of working or has died
▶ Fathers of one child

Is there any way to get out of military service?

Move to Mount Athos or have four or more children!

Greek law says that those residing in the monastic community of Mount Athos are not required to serve in the military. Also, Greek men do not have to serve in the military if they have four or more children; if they have serious health problems and are disabled or mentally ill; if their wife has died or is incapable of work and whose children cannot support themselves; and if they are the eldest son in a family whose members cannot support themselves.

What is more, men over the age of 45 do not have to serve in the military.

Can I buy my way out of military service?

No. But Greeks who are permanent residents abroad and over the age of 35 may pay 3,645 euros and serve only 45 days (instead of six months).

Can I at least choose where to serve?

No. It is widely rumoured, however, that Greek men with the right connections have secured service close to their home or in the branch (army, navy, airforce) of their choice.

Those who serve the reduced six months are usually assigned to the army.

Can I finish college/university before serving in the military?

Yes. You can request a temporary deferment.

The duration of the deferment is 5-6 years, just as long as you pass your courses.

Note: Deferments between six months and two years may be granted to Greek men who are in a drug addiction rehabilitation programme or who are undergoing therapy for a physical ailment. Also, Greek men whose brother is currently serving in the Greek military may request a deferment until he is discharged.

The defence minister also has the right to grant deferments for compelling social reasons.

As this book was going to print, officials at the defence ministry were discussing whether to stop granting deferments for educational purposes altogether.

What if I served in the Canadian Armed Forces?

If you served for six months or more, you will not be required to serve in the Greek military.

Note: this is also the case if you served in the military in other European Union countries and in the United States. Ask at the nearest Greek consulate for details.

What if I have a Greek last name? Will I be recruited if I visit Greece?

No, as long as you do not have a Greek passport or a Greek ID card. Having a Greek surname does not mean that you are automatically registered as a Greek citizen and thus required to serve in the military.

What about conscientious objectors?

They are required to complete alternative service (community service) that is 23 months long or unarmed military service that is 18 months long.

What about women?

Greek women are not obliged to serve in the military. They may, however, join as professionals.

How to get a permanent resident abroad certificate

The following documents must be submitted to Greek consulates:
▶ an application (available at the consulates)
▶ certificate of registration in Greece (usually from the municipality in Greece in which the applicant's parents married)
▶ School records, income tax returns and other official documents that cover each year from the applicant's tenth year of age until the time of the application
▶ All passports (valid and expired) in the applicant's possession
▶ A fee (about 10 euros)
More facts
▶ Basic training (boot camp) lasts six to seven weeks
▶ Those discharged from active service are placed in the reserves and are subject to periodic recall of 1-10 days at irregular intervals

❯ Draft dodgers residing in Greece cannot be issued a passport and cannot leave the country

❯ Until 2002, the passports of draft dodgers residing abroad were not renewed. Upon reentering Greece, these people were generally forced to conscribe. However, in 2002, the right was granted to all Greek citizens abroad to be issued passports, regardless of their draft status. In 2004, parliament granted partial amnesty to draft evaders, allowing them to visit Greece for up to 30 days in a single calendar year and for 40 days during a general election year (so that they can cast a ballot).

Countries with mandatory military service

Albania, Algeria, Angola, Armenia, Austria, Azerbaijan, Belarus, Bolivia, Bosnia and Herzegovina, Brazil, Bulgaria, Cambodia, Chile, Colombia, Croatia, Cuba, Cyprus, Czech Republic, Democratic People's Republic of Korea, Denmark, Dominican Republic, Ecuador, Egypt, Estonia, Ethiopia, Germany, Finland, France, Greece, Hungary, Iran, Iraq, Israel, Italy, Kazakhstan, Kuwait, Latvia, Lebanon, Lithuania, Madagascar, Mexico, Moldova, Mongolia, Mozambique, Norway, Panama, Paraguay, Philippines, Poland, Portugal, Romania, Russian Federation, Serbia, Slovakia, Slovenia, Spain, Sudan, Sweden, Switzerland, Tunisia, Turkey, Ukraine, Uzbekistan, Venezuela, Yemen, Zaire *(source www.mothersagainstthedraft.org)*

Information

❯ Check out the defence ministry's website *www. stratologia. gr* (it is currently under construction)

❯ Send a fax to the defence ministry 210-652-7106 or 210-654-5703

❯ Call your local recruitment office *(stratologiko grafeio)*. Ring the telephone directory 11888 for the nearest one

❯ If you reside abroad, contact your nearest Greek consulate

Greek men only:
Check if you have to serve in the Greek military

1) Are you a Greek citizen who was born and raised in Greece?

2) Are you the son of a Greek who was born and raised abroad and would like to reside in Greece (as a Greek citizen with a Greek ID card) permanently or for more than six months a year?

3) Are you the son of a Greek who moved abroad with your parents before your 11th birthday and now wish to reside in Greece (as a Greek citizen with a Greek ID card) permanently or for more than six months a year?

4) Are you a naturalised Greek citizen?

5) Do you reside in the monastic community of Mount Athos?

6) Are you the father of four or more children?

7) Are you physically disabled?

8) Are you mentally ill, suffering from any psychological disorder?

9) Have you been convicted of a serious crime?

10) Have both your parents died and do you have a sibling who is unmarried or incapable of working?

11) Are you a widower with a minor child or an adult child who is incapable of working?

▶ Get ready for boot camp if you answered yes to questions 1, 2, 3 or 4

▶ You're not obliged to serve in the Greek military if you answered yes to questions 5, 6, 7, 8, 9, 10 or 11

Greek Army Ελληνικός Στρατός
Greek Navy Ελληνικό Πολεμικό Ναυτικό
Greek Airforce Ελληνική Πολεμική Αεροπορία

Employment

Looking for a new job can be hard work, especially if you're far away from home and from your network of contacts and connections.

As an expatriate you will probably find yourself out of the corporate recruitment loop. Employers have no record of you, which means you are not visible on their executive radar.

That's why finding a job in Greece requires persistence and resourcefulness. So cast a wide net and start your search immediately. Consultants at various headhunters - executive search firms - in Athens agree that language is the biggest obstacle for expats trying to get their foot in the door.

"If you speak the language, it's not that difficult to find work," says Vergina Argiratou, human resource manager at Creme de la Creme, an executive recruitment agency in Athens. "If you don't speak Greek, you'll face problems."

But most expats have something that gives them an edge over the Greek competition. Their work experience abroad is considered an asset in the multinational business sector.

But this experience can sometimes get expats into trouble, especially if they try to work as they did abroad.

"Most foreigners are able to adapt easily to a new environment, which is very good," says Argiratou. "They also speak other foreign languages, which is also good, but they should try to be relaxed during the interview, though they should dress professionally for it," she adds.

Always remember that each country has its own interviewing behaviour and rules. What is very common and expected in England or in the United States may be extremely offensive to a Greek employer.

Some employers do not want to risk hiring and investing in someone who may decide to move back to his or her homeland, so Argaritou says expats should explain the reason why they moved to Greece. And those who do not speak Greek should tell the manager interviewing them that they are more than eager to learn.

According to one Canadian expat, who is employed as a human resource manager at a multinational company in Athens, job interviews here are nothing like back home. "There is a difference in the level of professionalism in both appearance and attitude," she told the *Athens News*. "You would not dream of going for a job interview wearing jeans in Canada. Here, people do."

"There is also a difference in the expectations," she adds. "There seems to be an assumption among the Greeks that if they have a university degree they are too good for entry-level positions."

Opportunities

Employment opportunities in the executive and managerial arenas are rather few. Opportunities are much better for marketing and managerial positions than they are for accounting because most expats are inexperienced in Greek tax laws. Teaching English or another foreign language is another possibility for expats, especially those without formal qualifications.

"How successful one is in finding a job really depends on the profession," says Julia Tanner, founding chairperson of the Thessaloniki Organisation for Women's Employment and Resources (TOWER) in northern Greece. "Obviously for anybody who is teaching English it is generally easy to get started. While the salary may not be very good, at least you can get a job. But if you are looking at other fields, it can be extremely difficult and frustrating. It's not always easy to get your qualifications recognised."

That's one reason why expats should be flexible. "Sometimes people end up doing something completely different, which can be frustrating," says Tanner. But there are cases where people persevered, such as a couple of people I know in the medical profession who are working in their own field."

Job ads

Learning about a vacancy is usually harder for expats who have not yet developed a network of contacts. That's why it is a good idea to contact recruitment companies so that your CV can be kept on file. It's easy, quick and free.

Another way to find out about employment opportunities is to check the classified section of the *Athens News* on Fridays and *Ta Nea* on Mondays. Job hunters should also pick up the *Hrysi Efkairia* - the country's largest-circulation classified newspaper - on Sundays.

Internet recruitment is another option. Online CV banks attract millions of people who want to put their skills on display for prospective employers around the world. The biggest online job posting site is *www. monster. com*

Expats in Greece may also visit the Greece-based site *www. skywalker.gr*

"I think you have to show a certain amount of initiative and not depend on what might be the obvious route to finding a job like looking in the newspapers because not all jobs get advertised," says Tanner. "It's always a good idea to network. That's one of the reasons why we've created TOWER."

The AZ of labour

▶ **Curriculum vitae (CV)** There are no strict rules for CVs in Greece. It should, however, be typed and not longer than three pages. A one-page cover letter should accompany the CV. It should explain why the person is an ideal candidate for the job. The letter should be signed.

▶ **Degree recognition** Greeks and foreigners who have completed university studies abroad must have their degrees officially recognised in order to pursue a career in the public sector. The Hellenic National Academic Recognition and Information Centre (DOATAP) is the official government body that validates foreign degrees. For details ring DOATAP on 210-528-1000 in Athens or 2310-379371 in Thessaloniki.

▶ **Labour inspectorate** The state-run labour inspectorate (SAPE) enforces legislation concerning working conditions, social security, safety and hygiene. Its job is to conduct inspections in the workplace and to impose fines in case of labour law violations. For more info or to file a complaint against your boss ring 210-883-5717 or 210-370-2358 in Athens or 2310-888721 in Thessaloniki.

▶ **Minimum wage** It's about 600 euros.

▶ **Public sector Law 2431/1996** provides access by European Union citizens to employment in the Greek public sector. However, the same law explicitly states that only Greek citizens have access to posts that imply direct or indirect participation in the exercise of public authority and involve duties, powers or responsibilities whose subject-matter is the safeguarding of the general interests of the state or other public sector institutions.

▶ **Rest** The minimum rest for any 24-hour period must not be less than 12 continuous hours. The maximum work week for waged and salaried workers may not exceed an average of 48 hours, including overtime, in a period of four months. Should the daily hours of work exceed six hours, there must be a break of at least 15 minutes during which employees have the right to leave their place of work. Employees should have at least one day (usually Sunday) off per week.

▶ **Right of association** All workers have a constitutional right to join or form a union.

▶ **Social insurance** The Greek social insurance system is split into a number of different funds for employed or self-employed persons. Each is governed by separate legislation. Insurance with these funds is compulsory. The majority of employed people belongs to the Social Insurance Foundation (IKA). The two other big insurance foundations are that for the self-employed (TEVE) and the Farmers' Pension Fund (OGA).

▶ **Sexual harassment** Parliament passed new legislation in August that defines sexual harassment at work for the first time and stipulates jail terms and substantial fines for offenders. The law provides for a prison sentence of between six months and three years for those convicted of sexual harassment, as well as a minimum fine of 1,000 euros. It also contains measures to combat discrimination against women at work and to promote equality. In a 2005 report, the World Economic Forum cited Greece as a European leader in gender inequality.

The European job mobility portal

What if ideal work for you is in another European country? One way to a new job in another European country is EURES (the European Job Mobility Portal). It's an online system that links jobseekers and employers in the European Union. The EURES databank includes thousands of vacancies. Open posts include positions in management and administration as well as chefs in France, pig stockpersons in Ireland and registered nurses in the UK. There are also thousands of curricula vitae (CVs) of EU citizens posted on its website for employers to scan.

EURES is a free service to both jobseekers and employers.

There are as many as one million job vacancies in 29 European countries posted on the EURES website (*http://europa.eu.int/eures*).

Employers may also search through nearly 10,000 CVs posted online.

There are as many as 10,000 Greek job vacancies posted on the EURES website.

The labour ministry's Organisation for the Employment of Human Resources (OAED) in Greece posts jobs on its website (*www.oaed.gr*).

Pensions

In a time of flux, ensuring you get the pension and benefits you've paid for all these years is becoming harder.

Things get even more complex when you work and contribute in one country and then decide to retire somewhere else. What happens then?

The *Athens News*, bearing in mind the complexity of social security legislation, is merely attempting to provide an overview of the situation rather than explain all the conditions and peculiarities pertaining to a great variety of specific cases.

Greece is bound by bilateral social insurance agreements with nine countries outside the European Union: the United States (since 1994), Canada (1983, including the province of Quebec, which has its own pension scheme), Argentina (1988), Brazil (1988), Venezuela (1995), Uruguay (1997), Switzerland (1975) and New Zealand (1994).

As for European Union citizens, a 1971 EU law ensures that people moving within the union do not lose their social security rights - sickness, maternity, old-age and widow/widower benefits. For instance, a Greek citizen who has worked in Italy for 10 years before returning to Greece is entitled to have that period of insurance or employment in Italy (as is the case in any other EU member states) taken into account.

An example: The agreement on social insurance between Canada and Greece, for instance, was signed in May 1981 and came into force in 1983. This accord, however, was replaced by another social insurance treaty signed in November 1995, which came into force in 1997. Based on this agreement, those who have contributed to both the Canadian and Greek social security systems may receive benefits from both countries based on periods they have lived or worked in Canada and Greece.

Social security agreements with other countries are based on similar principles.

Coordinating EU systems

An EU regulation coordinates systems in all member states. European Council regulation 1408/71 coordinates the national social insurance legislation of EU member states. It outlines "social security schemes to employed persons, to self-employed persons and to members of their families moving within the EU". Council regulation 574/72 lays down the framework for the implementation of the above regulation.

Regulation 1408/71, passed by the European Council in June 1971, ensures that people moving within the EU do not lose their social security rights, such as healthcare coverage and social security contributions. It also makes certain that people are not doubly liable for contributions.

This regulation applies to sick, maternity, invalidity, old-age and survivor's benefits, as well as benefits regarding accident at work and occupational diseases, unemployment and family benefits and death grants.

Regulation 1408/71 in practice

▶ A Greek citizen who works in France and wants to retire in Spain will be covered by the French social insurance system.

▶ A Greek citizen living in Germany and receiving unemployment benefits under German law wants to move back to Greece and work here but cannot afford to do so without receiving his unemployment benefits while he is looking for a job. According to regulation 1408/71, he may continue to draw benefits from one member state (in this case Germany) for up to three months after he had moved to another EU country.

▶ A Greek citizen who has worked in Italy for 10 years and wants to retire in Greece is entitled, according to regulation 1408/71, to have that period of insurance or employment in Italy (and any other EU country) taken into account in Greece.

Retiring abroad

Of interest to a large number of Greek pensioners (including non-Greek legal residents) who wish to retire abroad is whether the Greek pensions are payable in their countries of origin or in the country they wish to settle down in. According to labour ministry officials, this is only possible for those wishing to retire in an EU member state or in countries bound by a bilateral social insurance agreement with Greece.

There are four ways people in these specified countries may collect their Greek pensions:

❱ Monthly cheques (in the currency of that country) issued by the corresponding bank abroad and mailed to the pensioner's home

❱ Monthly payments directly deposited in a bank account opened by pensioners in the country where they are currently residing

❱ Pensioners may officially appoint someone in Greece to collect their pension

❱ Monthly payments may be deposited in a special savings account at the National Bank branch located at 3 Agorakritou St, Victoria Square. In this case, pensioners are required by law to submit an annual "certificate of life" - a signed statement stating that they are alive.

For more information

❱ Labour ministry's general secretariat for social insurance policy, department for bilateral agreements: 29 Stadiou St, Athens, tel 210-331-3153

❱ Central Pension Payment Office: 48 Agisilaou St, tel 210-527-9842

Online information

Have a question about your pension? The answer may be just a mouse-click away.

The European Commission has launched *EUlisses* (*http://ec. europa.eu/eulisses*) - a new website to give "easy access" to information about pension rights of citizens on the move in Europe.

According to the commission, this new online service is in demand. Seventy percent of all emails it receives each year has to do with social security and pension rights of workers switching jobs and countries.

"If you work for some years in Slovakia, then in Portugal and finally settle in Germany, every year you work, regardless of the country, counts for your pension claim," said Employment and Social Affairs Commissioner Vladimir Spidla. "When you reach retirement age, you get a pension that consists of all the partial pensions from the countries you have worked in. You don't lose a single cent."

The information on the website is currently available in seven languages (English, Greek, French, German, Dutch, Italian and Spanish), but will soon be updated in all 21 official EU languages.

The following are the most frequently asked questions by European citizens.

Questions and answers

Which countries are covered by EU rules coordinating social security?

Austria, Belgium, Bulgaria, the Czech Republic, Cyprus, Denmark, Estonia, Finland, France, Germany, Greece, Hungary, Ireland, Italy, Latvia, Lithuania, Luxembourg, Malta, the Netherlands, Poland, Portugal, Romania, Slovakia, Slovenia, the United Kingdom, Iceland, Liechtenstein, Norway and Switzerland.

Do the rules apply to non-EU citizens?

Within the EU, the rules also apply to nationals of third countries who have been legally residing in EU member states. However, European Free Trade Association countries Iceland, Liechtenstein, Norway and Switzerland will only recognise the retirement rules for their nationals and the 27 EU members.

I'm a pensioner. If I decide to live in another EU member state, will I still get my pension?

Yes. You can redirect your pension.

When can I retire if I have acquired pension rights in more than one European country where the retirement age differs?

You can apply to receive your pension once you have reached the legal retirement age in the country where you will claim your pension (usually the country where you reside).

If you have acquired pension rights in other European countries, you must have reached the legal retirement age of each country before you can claim your pension there. The social security institution in the country where you apply for your pension should also be made aware of the institutions in other European countries where you are claiming a pension.

Where should I pay my pension contributions?

In the country where you work. If you work there for less than a year, however, you will not be eligible for a pension. Your contributions only begin to count towards a pension after 12 months. The exception is if you are posted abroad for less than a year, in which case your employer will continue to pay pension contributions in your home country.

Can I get the pension contribution I have paid refunded if I go and live in another country?

Most countries (including Greece) will not refund your pension contributions if you move to another country.

Your contribution record is kept until you reach retirement age. This means that the contributions you have paid in one country can be neither transferred to another country nor repaid. When you retire, each country will pay you the part of your pension you have accumulated there.

What if I worked in an EU member-state before it became a member?

Your contributions will still be taken into account. The system is retroactive.

I live in one country and commute to work in another. Where should I apply for my pension?

In the country where you live. The pension institution in that country will forward your pension application to the other European countries where you have accumulated pension rights - including the country where you work.

How do I apply for a pension if I have lived and/or worked in more than one European country?

You should apply in the country where you are now living (once you approach the legal retirement age there). The pension institution should send you all the necessary documents for your pension claim about four months before you reach retirement age. In processing your pension claim, the institution is also responsible for collating your records from all the other countries where you have built up periods of insurance cover.

How is my pension calculated?

If you worked long enough in a country to qualify for a full pension, you can claim that pension from anywhere in the EU. (If, in addition, you worked for at least a year in a second EU country, your full pension from one country does not prevent you from claiming a partial pension from another country as well).

If you have not worked for a full pension in any one EU country, each country in which you paid contributions for at least one year will have to pay you a partial pension.

Each country's pension institution calculates your pension according to its own rules based on the contributions that you have paid, and deposits your pension directly into your bank account.

If, at any point, you were insured in a country for less than a year, the country where you last worked or lived may take those periods into account.

Making a will

It's not just for the rich. Making a will is the easiest way to ensure that all your worldly goods - from your priceless antiques to your canoe and luxury yacht - are passed on to family and friends as you wish.

Dying intestate

If you die without a will, all your assets will be divided amongst your family according to the law. According to Greek law, in the absence of a will the surviving spouse comes into a quarter of the inheritance, while the deceased's children will share the remaining three-quarters. If there is no surviving spouse, the children stand to inherit everything. If there are no children, the surviving spouse is entitled to half of the inheritance; the other half will go to the siblings or the parents of the deceased.

If there are no apparent heirs, the entire inheritance passes to the state.

Death duty According to Greek law, those who inherit from a person who died after 1983 are required to pay inheritance tax to the Greek state. In the case of real estate, heirs are taxed on the objective value and not on the market value (which is usually much higher).

The taxation rate on inherited assets depends on the relationship of the heirs to the deceased. Athens-based lawyer Christos Iliopoulos explains:

1. Spouses, children, grandchildren and parents of the deceased are exempt from paying tax for the first 80,000 euros. The tax is 5 percent on the next 20,000 euros and 10 percent on the next 120,000 euros after that. For instance, tax on an estate worth 220,000 euros would be 13,000 euros. For amounts exceeding 220,000 euros, heirs are taxed at 20 percent.

2. Grandparents, great-grandchildren, siblings, nieces,

nephews, step-parents, children from a previous marriage and in-laws are taxed differently. They are exempt from paying inheritance tax for amounts up to 15,000 euros. For the next 45,000 euros, the tax is 10 percent; for the 160,000 euros after the rate is 20 percent. So tax on an estate worth 220,000 euros would come to 36,500 euros. For amounts exceeding 220,000 euros, these heirs are taxed at 30 percent.

3. Other relatives and persons not related to the deceased are exempt from inheritance tax only on the first 5,000 euros. They are taxed at 20 percent for the next 55,000 euros and 30 percent for the next 160,000 euros. So, tax on an estate worth 220,000 euros comes to 59,000 euros. For amounts exceeding 220,000 euros, these heirs are taxed at 40 percent. Note: All heirs are required, by law, to declare their inheritance to the Greek tax authorities within six months (or 12 months if they are permanent residents abroad). If they do not, they will be subject to a fine.

The making of a will in Greece

Everyone - over the age of 18 and of sound mind and memory - who resides or owns property in Greece has the right to make a will. This includes the tens of thousands of expatriates who purchase a summer or retirement home in Greece. Few Greeks, however, decide to make a will. Those who do are generally older or seriously ill.

"People of other nationalities, like Britons, are more willing to make a will at younger ages," says Iliopoulos. "Greeks tend to wait until they are very old to make a will."

Athens lawyer Christos Iliopoulos answers our questions on making a will in Greece:

Why should a person make a will?

No one has to make a will. You should make a will if your wishes are different from what Greek law prescribes after your death. So, you should first find out what the law says. If you are not happy with that, you can make a will to change it. However, this does not mean that you are completely free to change the law because there are some stipulations which must be strictly adhered to and cannot change. For instance, you cannot completely leave out your children and your spouse. They are always entitled to a proportion of the inheritance. There are extreme cases, however, in which you can disinherit them, like if they tried to kill you.

Article 1822 of Greece's inheritance law explicitly states that a spouse - a rightful heir - may only be deprived of his or her inheritance if the deceased had filed for divorce and if the grounds for the divorce are "well-founded". According to article 1840 of the same legislation, there are five legal causes for disinheriting rightful heirs:

1. If they tried to kill the testator or his or her spouse, children or close family member

2. If they caused intentional physical harm to the testator or his or her spouse physical injury

3. If they are convicted of a crime or a serious misdemeanour against the testator or his or her spouse

4. If they failed to pay alimony or child support as ordered by the law

5. If they live a violent, immoral or unethical life, against the testator's will.

How does one make a will?

There are three types of wills. One is the so-called handwritten will. You can write anything you want on any kind of document. It can even be a letter expressing your wishes. Of course, this is an informal process and the chances are that it will require interpretation. The second is a secret will. It's basically the same as a handwritten one, but you put it in a sealed envelope and give it to a notary public for safekeeping. It is opened after the person dies. The third is a public will. To make this will, you go to a notary public, who writes the will and keeps it on file. Note: The advantage of the secret and handwritten will is that no one - not even those who were called to witness the signing of the will and, of course, not the rightful heirs - know what is in the will.

What should be included in a will?

Basically, a will should indicate how a person's property will be distributed after death: who will inherit the property and assets. This includes any kind of possessions, including things that may or may not have a monetary value, but sentimental value. Note: intellectual property is also included. This means that an author can name a literary executor.

Can a person state in their will that someone is only conditionally entitled to the inheritance, for instance if he/she graduates from university or gets married?

Yes. This is a donation under a precondition. However, the precondition cannot be something that is illegal or against accepted morals.

Can a beloved pet inherit a person in Greece?

No, I don't think this can happen in Greece.

Can a person update or change his/her will?

Yes. It can be done. If there is more than one will, the most recent one prevails. It is not necessary to have destroyed the previous will.

Does marriage or divorce affect a will?

If, at the time of death a person is married, his or her spouse has certain rights. If at the time of the death, the person is no longer married, the ex-spouse has no right at all.

What if the will was written when they were married?

In this case, we will probably need to interpret the will because if the deceased said in the will that he wishes to leave something to his wife, but later there was a divorce, we have to interpret whether he wanted to give it to the specific person or to this person because she was his wife. It's best to include a clause in the will stating what will happen in case of a divorce.

Can a baby inherit?

Yes. Anyone, regardless of his/her age, may inherit.

Can a will be challenged?

Anybody can challenge a will if they can prove to a court that the deceased was not of sound mind when he made his will. Or, they can argue that the deceased was under threat. It is up to the court to decide.

Is it easier to challenge a handwritten will?

Yes, because unlike a handwritten will, a public will is made before a notary public. Even though the notary is not a doctor, the notary has the common sense to realise whether that person is of a sound mind or not.

How much does it cost to make a will?

It depends on how much the lawyer wants. There is no limit. The price, however, depends on how complicated the will is. It may cost as little as few hundred euros. However, a lawyer is not always necessary. The services of a notary public are necessary in the case of a public or secret will.

Is a will written in English and approved by a British notary acceptable in Greece?

Yes, this will is acceptable (and enforceable) in Greece as long as it has first been probated in the UK. The validity of the will depends on whether a British notary may legally prepare/approve will documents as per UK law. Following this procedure, a certified will (as probated in UK) can be registered (probated) with the Athens Court of First Instance (department of wills) so that the beneficiaries may inherit and formally register any Greek estate etc which is mentioned in the will.

What happens if a couple is not legally married?

If a couple is not legally married, the surviving partner may only inherit by virtue of a will (specifically naming him/her as the beneficiary). The imposed taxation is higher in such cases. Of course, the validity of such a provision may depend on various other factors, such as whether the deceased's closest relatives (who have a rightful share to the inheritance) have been honoured.

Can the "handwritten" will be written in a language other than Greek?

Yes, a will written in a language other than Greek is valid, provided of course that all other prerequisites and conditions of its validity (as stipulated by the Greek Civil Code) are respected.

The transfer of property (*metavivasi akiniton*): Instead of making a will, many Greek parents choose to transfer property rights to their children before their death in order to take advantage of tax-friendly legislation.

Under current law, the "donation" of property to children (regardless of their age) by their parents is either tax-free or subject to a significantly reduced tax. The parents, however, retain the rights to the property until they die.

Fast facts

▶ The children and surviving spouse are always entitled to a portion of the inheritance, no matter what the will states, unless they have done something very serious to warrant their disinheritance

▶ The beneficiaries (according to the will) and close relatives of the deceased (if there is no will) are required to attend a special court hearing (*klironomitirio*) where a judge will legally declare them beneficiaries and state their portion of the inheritance. Or, they can simply sign an "acceptance of inheritance" (*apodohi klironomias*) before a notary public

▶ In the case of immovable property (land, house, apartment), the heirs must register it at the local public registry (*ypothikofylakio*)

Greece's three wills

1 According to Greek inheritance law, a holographic (handwritten) will must be written entirely by the person making the will. It must be dated and signed. Any additions and changes to the will must also be signed by the person to be considered valid. Crossing out something or changing it without initialling it will render the will null and void. The handwritten will may be kept anywhere by the testator (the person making the will) or may be given to a notary public for safekeeping.

2 A public will is written by a notary public and signed by the testator. The signing of the will must take place before the notary public and three witnesses or before two notaries and one witness. Note: a witness cannot be someone who stands to inherit or someone who is blind or deaf or under age 18. If the will is more than one page long, every page must be signed. The notary public must read the will out loud before the testator signs it. If the testator is deaf, he/she must be given a copy to read. If the testator is deaf and illiterate, the will must be drafted and signed before five witnesses or before two notaries and three witnesses. If the testator is not fluent in Greek, an interpreter must be present.

3 With a secret will, the testator must sign it before a notary public and three witnesses or two notaries and one witness. The secret will is not read out loud by the notary. This means that only people who can read may make a secret will.

Across Europe

Conflicting laws in England, Spain and France

Inheritance law varies from country to country and may be contradictory, causing confusion. In Greece, the children, spouse and parents of the deceased are always entitled to a share of the inheritance. In England, you are free to dispose of your estate as you wish. In Spain, however, two-thirds of the inheritance goes to the closest heirs (a third of that portion must go to the surviving spouse). The remaining may be distributed freely. In France, inheritance law divides the property in strict order: 1) children; 2) parents, siblings, nephews and nieces; 3) grandparents; 4) spouse; 5) uncles, aunts, cousins and other relatives.

Article 28 of the Greek Civil Code states that "inheritance relations are governed by the law of the citizenship which the deceased had when he died". This means that if a French national dies and leaves property in Greece, it is French law which will determine who inherits and what share. Greek law will only determine how much inheritance tax will be paid to the Greek state by the heirs. But who are the heirs will be decided by French law.

Another example: a UK citizen residing in Greece may write his/her will (handwritten, public or secret) in Greece. However, how the deceased's assets are distributed will be based on British inheritance law rather than Greek legislation. In England, you are free to dispose of your estate as you wish.

In France and the United Kingdom, it is the location of the property and not the nationality or permanent residence of the owner which determines how property will be distributed after the owner's death. As is the case in Greece, Spanish law states that succession of all property, whether movable or immovable and wherever situated, is determined by the law of the deceased's nationality.

The EU is trying to clear the heir

Let's say a person who has lived in a European Union member state other than her or his own for several years dies in that country. All the heirs live in another EU member state and most of the property that they stand to inherit is in yet another EU state. Which EU country's inheritance law applies if the deceased did not leave a will? It's a difficult question to answer.

That is why the European Commission published a Green Paper discussing the process regarding intestate (in the absence of a will) and testate succession in cases where there is an international dimension. This will be the basis for future common EU policy, if all member states agree. "The growing mobility of people in an area without internal frontiers and the increasing frequency of unions between nationals of different member states, often entailing the acquisition of property in the territory of several EU member states, are a major source of complication in succession to estates, " says the European Commission in its 11-page Green Paper. "The difficulties facing those involved in a transnational succession mostly flow from the divergence in substantive rules, procedural rules and conflict rules in the member states."

According to the European Commission, it may be a good idea to allow the future deceased to choose the law applicable to his/her succession, with or without the agreement of his/her heirs. The commission is also proposing the creation of central EU-wide register of wills.

What is more, the commission is seeking to establish EU legislation that would "simplify matters for heirs by allowing the recognition and enforcement of documents needed for the recognition of their rights". Another question raised is what happens in the case of simultaneous death. The order in which two people who are likely to inherit each other's property die can have an impact on their respective heirs' rights.

"Where people die in the same incident, some member states presume that they died at the same time, whereas others presume that they died in particular order," says the Green Paper. "If their successions are governed by different laws, it may be impossible to administer them."

Rights and obligations of EU citizens

Citizens of the European Union enjoy the freedom of movement to all EU member states (Austria, Belgium, Bulgaria, Cyprus, the Czech Republic, Denmark, Estonia, Finland, France, Germany, Greece, Hungary, Ireland, Italy, Latvia, Lithuania, Luxembourg, Malta, the Netherlands, Poland, Portugal, Romania, Slovakia, Slovenia, Spain, Sweden and the United Kingdom). Free movement is a cornerstone of EU citizenship.

Citizens of Bulgaria and Romania (the two newest countries to join the EU in January 2007) will be subject to a two-year transitional period in Greece. This means that they will be denied free access to Greece's labour market. They will be subject to the same rules and regulations that apply to non-EU immigrants.

In January 2007, the labour ministry announced that Romanians and Bulgarians will enjoy free access to the Greek labour market, provided that they can prove at least 12 months of legal residence in Greece.

Residence for EU citizens

Those eligible for residence in another member state include students, pensioners, workers and those who can financially support themselves, as well as non-EU nationals married to EU citizens. A residence permit is not required by law for those who wish to stay in Greece up to three months. Non-Greek EU citizens who wish to live and/or work in Greece require an EU residence permit.

The application procedure for the residence permit is relatively trouble-free. The health certificate requirement was scrapped several years ago. The permit is issued on the spot. The residence permit also serves as a work permit.

Note: The European Parliament approved new rules to scrap the residence permit requirement for European Union nationals living in another member state. European Union Council directive (2004/58/EC) eliminates the need for EU citizens to obtain a residence permit. According to the directive, EU member states may simply require EU citizens to register with local authorities. The new directive is intended to boost the free movement of EU citizens within the union. It is also aimed at reducing bureaucracy.

The application procedure for a five-year-duration EU residence permit

When to file: Within three months of one's stay in Greece.

Where to file: Applications for residence permits are submitted to the nearest aliens' bureau. In Athens it is located at 24 Petrou Ralli St.

Application requirements for pensioners or those in Greece for work purposes

▶ A passport or identification card
▶ Three passport-size photographs
▶ A document (utility or telephone bill is accepted) stating their home address
▶ An official document proving they are receiving a pension. Or a work contract signed by their employer and validated by the local labour inspectorate. Or proof they are self-employed in Greece

Application requirements for students
▶ A valid passport or ID
▶ Three passport-size photographs
▶ A document verifying the applicant is enrolled at a school recognised by the Greek state

Application requirements for family members of EU citizens
▶ A valid passport or ID
▶ A certificate issued by authorities in the applicant's home

country stating their relation to the EU citizen already in Greece
▶ Three passport-size photographs
Renewing the residence permit
The residence permit is valid for up to five years and must be renewed at least two weeks before it expires. The application procedure is the same with the procedure for the issuing of the initial permit. Only one passport-size photograph is needed.

Application requirements for citizens of Bulgaria and Romania who have been residing legally in Greece for at least one year

▶ A valid passport or identification card
▶ A document issued by the applicant's local prefecture indicating the duration of his/her legality in Greece (the number of years he/she has held a valid work/residence permit)
▶ Three passport-size photographs
▶ A document indicating the applicant's permanent residence or a statutory declaration (*ypefthyni dilosi*) signed by the applicant and validated by the police
▶ A statutory declaration (*ypefthyni dilosi*) signed by the applicant, stating that he/she has medical insurance
▶ A work contract validated by the labour inspectorate. If self-employed, the applicant must submit a document issued by the tax office stating the launch of his/her business and a photocopy of his/her receipt booklet.
Special cases
(EU citizens who work in Greece do not need a residence permit if they travel to their home in another member state either on a daily basis or at least once a week.
▶ Authorities may reject an application if they deem the applicant poses a threat to public health or public order. This decision can be appealed. Note: During the first three months you only need your identity card or passport. If you wish to

stay for a longer period, you need a residence card, not as a prerequisite for being able to live in the new country, but as a proof of your rights in this country. Another reason for the residence card lies in statistical research as regards movement of population.

Info

For further information ring police headquarters in Athens on 210-340-5969 or contact your local police station (ask for the *tmima allodapon*).

▶ If you live in western Athens, ring 210-531-9315 or go to the police station in Egaleo (21 Marmara St).

▶ If you reside in southeastern Attica (from Ilioupoli to Vari), ring 210-969-0299. The police station is located at the former Athens airport (Anatoliko) in Glyfada.

▶ If you reside in northern Attica ring 210-687-5176. The police station is located at 15 Agiou Orous St in Maroussi.

Rights and obligations of non-EU citizens

The Greek parliament passed new immigration legislation (law 3386/2005) in August 2005. It forms the cornerstone of Greece's immigration policy. As was the case with the country's previous immigration law (2910/2001), the new law outlines the procedure non-European Union nationals must follow when seeking to enter the country for work purposes. Below are several key features of the new law.

Types of residence permits

The new law creates more than 30 different types of residence permits, corresponding to different reasons a holder wishes to stay in Greece. There is a residence permit for work purposes (salaried employment, self-employment, seasonal work, corporate executives, athletes/coaches and members of foreign archaeology schools in Greece). There is also a permit for immigrants who wish to pursue independent economic activities or to invest in Greece. Permits are granted for study purposes, vocational training and to foreign press journalists, spiritual leaders (of known religions), tour group leaders, researchers and adult children of foreign diplomats. Residence permits, under the new law, may also be issued in "exceptional" circumstances, ie on humanitarian grounds and in so-called public interest cases. Special residence permits are issued to immigrant family members of legal residents (Greeks, EU citizens and immigrants already legally residing in Greece). There are also two types of permanent residence permits. One is permanent (issued after 10 years of legal residence). The other is a five-year-duration permit (renewable automatically) for longterm residents, based on a European Union directive.

Note: All residence permits may also serve as work permits, if so indicated. This means immigrants do not have to apply for a separate work permit.

General conditions for the right to stay

Immigrants who enter the country legally and who hold a valid passport or other travel document have the right to stay in Greece unless they pose a threat to national security and public order. At the end of each month, authorities at local regional offices (*periferia*) compile a list containing the names of immigrants who renewed their residence permit the previous month. The list is forwarded to the public order ministry where officials check that the immigrants do not have a criminal record.

Would-be immigrants may be denied the right to enter or stay in the country if they are deemed a threat to public health. Once in Greece, however, immigrants who fall ill will not face deportation. All immigrants legally living in Greece must have medical insurance.

Applications for the issuing and renewal of residence permits:

According to the law, applicants are required to submit their application (and all required documents, including a fee) to their local municipality. Immigrants will then be issued a document certifying that they have done so. The holder of this document, known as the *veveosi* in Greek, is considered legal in the country while the authorities examine his/her application.

By law, officials have two months by which to examine the application and render a decision.

Future labour migration

A special committee to track labour market demand has been created at each local regional office (*periferia*) nationwide. The local regional general secretary and representatives from the labour inspectorate, the labour ministry's organisation for the employment of human resources, the local labour centre, and the general confederation of Greek farmers' associations and the union of agricultural cooperatives sit on the committee.

The committee meets in December of every second year. It is responsible for recording vacancies in the labour market that can be filled by would-be immigrants. This information is forwarded to the ministers of labour and interior, who decide how many new residence permits Greece will issue for work purposes each year. The local regional offices, the Organisation for the Employment of Human Resources (OAED) and consulates abroad are then notified.

Greek consulates are responsible for publicising the recorded employment vacancies abroad. Would-be immigrants wishing to come to Greece to work submit applications to the consulate. A detailed list of the applicants is then forwarded to regional offices in Greece in the final three months of each year.

Back in Greece, employers seeking to hire immigrant workers are allowed to view the list and select the applicants they wish to hire. The local regional general secretary makes the final decision. Would-be immigrants who enter into an employment contract with a Greek employer are permitted to come to Greece. They are issued a temporary three-month-duration visa by the Greek consulate in their home country. Once in Greece, they have one month by which to apply for a one-year-duration residence permit. This permit is renewable for two years.

Seasonal workers

Immigrants are allowed to enter the country for seasonal work (up to six months per calendar year). They are employed by a specific employer. They are not allowed to renew their temporary residence permit. Note: Seasonal work is an issue regulated by bilateral agreements between Greece and other countries.

Issuing and renewal of residence permits for immigrants who intend to start their own employment

Immigrants are allowed to enter the country with the intention of creating their own employment. They must fulfil two conditions:
- Sufficient funds to start the employment (at least 60,000 euros deposited in a bank)
- The employment activity must contribute to the growth of the national economy

The application for a residence permit is submitted to the local regional office (*periferia*). It must be accompanied by a comprehensive business plan. Unsuccessful applicants will be allowed to reapply after one year.

Residence for immigrants who intend to invest in Greece

Immigrants are permitted to enter the country with the intention of investing in Greece. To do so, they are required to show how they plan to invest and to prove they have sufficient capital (300,000 euros or more deposited in a Greek bank). The investment must also create at least 10 new jobs (30 percent of which will be filled by Greeks). Immigrants are required to submit an application and a business plan to their nearest Greek consulate. The application is forwarded to the interior ministry's immigration office where it is reviewed. The final decision is made by the interior minister.

If approved, the residence permit, which is issued by the interior minister, is valid for three years and renewed for three years each time.

Immigrant students

Immigrants are allowed to enter the country for study purposes. They are required to prove enrolment at a Greek state university, technical college or any other public institute of higher education. The residence permit issued to students is valid for one year and is renewable each year. They are allowed to stay one extra year to learn the Greek language.

Residence for those who are well-to-do

Immigrants who can financially support themselves without having to work in Greece (pensioners and financially independent) are eligible for a one-year-duration residence permit, renewable each year. They are required to prove they can cover the cost of their living expenses in Greece. Other application requirements include proof they do not have a criminal record and posses a clean bill of health. They must also have health and medical coverage.

Residence in special cases

The ministers of interior and labour have the right to grant residence permits on "humanitarian grounds" to immigrants who are seriously injured in work-related and other accidents, as well as those who are victims of violent crimes or who suffer from a debilitating illness. The permit, which will also serve as a work permit, will be valid for one year and is renewable each year. No application fee is required.

Family reunification

Immigrants legally residing in Greece for at least two years are allowed to bring their spouse and children to Greece, provided they fulfil the following conditions:
 ❯ proof of family relations (marriage certificate, birth certificate)
 ❯ proof the family members will reside with them
 ❯ stable and sufficient personal income
Immigrants are only allowed to bring their spouse (over age 18) and dependent children (under age 21).

In the case of polygamy - the custom of being married to more than one person at a time - immigrants are not allowed to bring more than one spouse to Greece.

The application for family reunification is examined by the local regional general secretary. If approved, the Greek consulate abroad will issue the family members a special entry visa. They will then be eligible for a residence permit valid for one year and renewable for two years. Once in Greece, family-based immigrants will have the right to education and access to the labour market. The spouse will be allowed to secure his/her own residence permit in the case of marital separation, divorce or death of the spouse. The minor children will have this right on their 21st birthday.

Family of Greeks or EU citizens Immigrants (citizens of countries outside the EU) who are married to, or are the children (under age 21) of, Greek or EU citizens will be allowed to reside and work in Greece. Applicants are required to show a valid passport and a document verifying their relation with the Greek or EU citizen. In some cases, they will also be required to undergo a health exam to prove they do not suffer from a contagious disease. The permit is valid for five years and may also serve as a work permit. No application fee is required. They are allowed to apply for permanent residence after five years.

Longterm resident status

Immigration law 3386/2005 outlines provisions in compliance with European Council Directive (2003/109/EC) on longterm resident status of third-country nationals (non-EU immigrants). The purpose of this EU directive is to grant immigrants the status of longterm residents after five years of legal residence on the territory of a member state. According to the law, all adult immigrants who have legally resided in Greece for at least five years will be able to secure the status of longterm resident. Immigrants are required to prove at least five years of legal residence as of September 2001.

They will also be required to fulfil the following conditions:
▶ sufficient and stable personal income
▶ health insurance
▶ fluency in the Greek language and knowledge of Greek history and culture
▶ high moral standards and a strong character

Note: Eligibility for this longterm resident status does not apply to immigrants in Greece for study or vocational training purposes. Immigrants who remained outside Greece for more than 10 months during the five-year period will not be eligible.

To demonstrate fluency in the Greek language, applicants must successfully complete an advanced-level Greek-language course, designated as level four out of four, administered by the education ministry's Institute for Lifelong Education (IDEKE). A July 2006 presidential decree explicitly states that immigrants who wish to secure this new status must first complete a 100-hour level-four course and a 25-hour course in Greek history and culture. A certificate will be issued upon passing a final exam. IDEKE also offers level 1-3 courses. Level 1 is for beginners - immigrants who do not speak a word of Greek. Level four is for immigrants who are fluent in the language, meaning they can converse in the language, read and write with ease at the secondary school level.

All lessons are free.

Note: Immigrants are not required to complete levels 1 through 3 before enrolling in the level-four course. They may sit a special test that will determine their Greek language abilities. Those who are fluent in the language may go directly to level four. Immigrants who have successfully completed middle or secondary school in Greece are not required to take Greek lessons or to sit the level-four examination.

The 'ensima'

Proof of stable employment and social insurance remains the main stipulation for the renewal of the residence permit. Immigrants are required to produce a specific number of days' worth of social insurance stamps (ensima). In January 2006, the government fixed the minimum number of ensima that non-European Union immigrants in Greece need to renew their residence permit. Immigrant workers insured with IKA (the country's biggest social insurance foundation) need at least 200 days' worth of ensima per year. Immigrants who are insured with the OGA (the farmers' pension fund) need to prove legal employment and social insurance contributions for 150 days or more. Immigrants who are insured with IKA, but who have more than one employer, also need at least 150 days of social insurance coverage to renew their residence permit. Such is the case for construction workers, domestic workers, caregivers for the elderly and baby-sitters).

Immigrants are allowed to purchase up to 20 percent of the ensima they need.

However, immigrants who are members of the board, directors or managers of a company in Greece have only to prove they are registered with a social insurance foundation and have medical insurance and pharmaceutical coverage. The same applies for athletes and trainers, as well as members of artistic groups and foreign archaeological schools.

Application fees

Below are the application fees, as outlined in law 3386/2005, for the issuing and renewal of the residence permit:

▶ 150 euros for a one-year permit
▶ 300 euros for a two-year permit
▶ 450 euros for a three-year permit
▶ 900 euros for the permit issued to longterm residents

(a special EU-wide permit automatically renewable every five years)

▶ 900 euros for permanent permits (issued to immigrants after 10 years of legal residence)

Note: the application is free for the children (under age 14) of immigrants

The rights of non-EU nationals legally residing in Greece

▶ The right to social security and membership in trade unions

▶ The right to travel abroad and re-enter the country, provided that their residence permit has not expired upon returning to Greece

▶ Children of immigrants have the right to education. They are also allowed to enrol in public school, even if their parents are undocumented

Obligations

▶ Immigrants are obliged to submit their application for the issuing and renewal of their residence permit in person or they may authorise a proxy to do so on their behalf

▶ Immigrants are obliged to notify authorities if they change address and if they marry, divorce or have a child. They must also notify authorities if they lose their passport or are in the process of renewing it and if they lose their residence permit. The same applies if they change employers or end a work contract

▶ Immigrants are obliged to leave the country immediately if authorities deny their application for a residence permit

Administrative deportation

Immigrants have five days by which to appeal an administrative deportation order issued against them. The public order minister has three days to decide on the matter. If deportation is impossible because of conditions in the country of origin, the public order minister has the right to allow the immigrant to remain in Greece with restrictions. The law prohibits the deportation of minors, the elderly (over age 80) and the parents of children who are legal residents in Greece. Exceptions, however, are made if a person is deemed a serious threat to public order and public health. Immigrants are required to pay the cost of deportation (transport and detention). The cost is covered by the state if they do not have the necessary funds.

Illegal immigration

▶ Immigrants who enter the country illegally face three months in prison and a fine of 1,500 euros. If an immigrant is a fugitive or owes money to the state and is caught trying to flee the country, he/she faces at least six months in prison and a fine of more than 3,000 euros.

▶ Employers are not allowed to hire an immigrant without a residence permit. If they do, they will face a three-month prison sentence and a fine between 3,000 and 15,000 euros for each undocumented migrant they had working for them. They may also be forced to cover the cost of deportation. The local regional general secretary may also decide to close the business, shop or nightclub for up to 12 months.

▶ In the case of undocumented migrants being forced into prostitution, the person charged with deriving income from this illegal activity faces more than two years in prison and a fine of more than 6,000 euros; or more than three years in prison and at least 15,000 euros in fines if the migrant victim is a minor.

▶ Employers who hire or fire (legal) immigrant workers must notify their local regional office (periferia) each time.

▶ It is illegal to rent a home to an immigrant who does not hold a passport or a valid travel document or an entry visa or a residence permit

▶ Hotels, clinics and hospitals are required to notify the police each time they serve an immigrant

Those who do not comply with the above requirements are subject to a fine between 1,500 and 3,000 euros.

▶ Those charged with facilitating the illegal entry of immigrants into Greece face a five-month prison sentence and a fine of at least 3,000 euros. Those charged with facilitating the stay or harbouring an undocumented immigrant face a fine of 3,000 euros and at least six months in prison. The same applies to an immigrant who tries to enter the country with a fake passport

▶ Motorists, captains and pilots charged with facilitating the illegal entry of immigrants face up to a year in prison and a fine between 5,000 and 20,000 euros for each immigrant. The fine reaches 100,000 euros if people's lives were put at risk

The application form

The first step to applying for a residence permit is to obtain a four-page application form, available at municipalities nationwide.

The application form contains some questions that are not directly related to the issuing or renewal of the residence permit. The government is seeking to collect statistics to furnish the European Union's statistical agency (Eurostat).

Below is an unofficial English translation of the application form available only in Greek:

Page 1 - Personal details

Section I: Indicate the prefecture and region responsible for examining your application and issuing your residence permit. Indicate your local municipality or village council

Section II: To be completed and signed upon submitting your application

Section III: Indicate the reason for your residence in Greece. Studies, salaried employment etc. Also, mark an X in one of the five boxes:

❯ First-time issuing of residence permit
❯ Renewal of residence permit
❯ Re-issuing (in case the permit was lost, stolen, destroyed)
❯ New issuing (in case the permit had been revoked)
❯ Change of personal details
Section IV: Personal details

A1) Surname (in Latin characters, as it appears in your passport)

A2) Given name (in Latin characters, as it appears in your passport)

A3) Father's given name (in Latin characters)

A4) Father's surname (in Latin characters)

A5) Mother's given name (in Latin characters)

A6) Mother's surname (in Latin characters)

A7) Date of birth (date/month/year)

A8) Country of birth

A9) Gender (male / female)

A10) Nationality / citizenship

A11) Mark X in box if you are stateless (no nationality)

A12) Mark X in box if you have applied for Greek citizenship through naturalisation

A13) Tax roll number (AFM)

A14) Indicate your local tax office

A15) Social insurance number (AMA)

A16) Indicate your social insurance foundation (IKA, TEVE or OGA)

Page 2 - Declaration of circumstances
Section B

B1) Indicate whether you hold a passport, a *laissez-passer* document (a travel document issued in exceptional cases) or any other travel document

B2) The number of your travel document

B3) Expiry date of your travel document

B4) Country issuing your travel document (in Greek letters)

Section Γ

Γ1) Your street (in Greek letters)

Γ2) Your address number

Γ3) Postal code

Γ4) Municipality or village

Γ5) Prefecture

Γ6) Phone number (work/home/mobile)

Section Δ

If you have been issued a residence permit, indicate

Δ1) Issuing authority of your permit (police, regional office, OAED)

Δ2) Indicate the type of document (Green Card, a sticker in your passport or a permit issued by the police)

Δ3) If applicable, indicate the number appearing on the sticker in your passport

Δ4) Indicate the number of your immigration register number (*mitro-ou*)

Δ5) Indicate the number of your permit

Δ6) Indicate what type of permit it is (was it issued for work purposes, study purposes, family reunification etc)

Δ7) Date of issue and expiry (date/month/year)

Δ8) Mark X in the box if you are the holder of a residence permit

Δ9) Is your name included as a dependent on a residence permit issued to your parent or spouse? If so, mark X in the appropriate box (parent/spouse)

Δ10) Mark X in the box if you are a recognised refugee

Δ11) Marx X in the box if you are staying in Greece on the basis of 'international protection' or so-called humanitarian grounds

Δ12) Marx X in the box if you are an asylum-seeker (if you have applied for asylum)

Δ13) Marx X in the box if you have applied for the so-called humanitarian grounds

Δ14) I had a residence permit that expired on -(date)-

Δ15) Mark X in the box if you have never held a residence permit

Δ16) If applicable, indicate the date your application for asylum or 'international protection' on so-called humanitarian protection was rejected by authorities

Δ17) If applicable, indicate the date your entry visa expired

Δ18) Indicate the date you entered Greece (date/month/year)

Section E

E1a) Mark X in the box if you are single

E1b) Mark X in the box if you are married

E1c) Mark X in the box if you are divorced

E1d) Mark X in the box if you are a widow/widower

E2) Indicate the number of your minor children: in Greece and abroad

E3) Indicate the number of adult children: in Greece and abroad

Section ST

Indicate your country of residence before coming to Greece. Information to include: country, date of residence, with or without residence permit

Section Z

Z1) Do you plan on living in Greece permanently? Mark X in the appropriate box (Yes/No)

Z2) Do you wish to move to another country? Mark X in the appropriate box (Yes/No)

Z3) If you do wish to move to another country, indicate which

Page 3 - Family living with you

Section H

H1) Family relation

H2) Surname

H3) Name

H4) Father's name

H5) Father's surname

H6) Mother's name

H7) Mother's surname

H8) Date of birth (date/month/year)

H9) Country of birth

H10) Gender (male/female)

H11) If applicable, indicate the number of the residence permit in their passport

H12) Indicate the number of their passport

H13) Indicate the expiry date of their passport

H14) Indicate the country that issued their passport

H15) Indicate whether you wish to include their name on your residence permit (Yes/No)

Page 4 - Employment, financial details and education

Section Θ

Θ1) Mark X in box if you are employed

Θ2) Mark X in box if you are unemployed

Θ3) Mark X in box if you are collecting unemployment benefits

Θ4) Type of employment (indicate using one of the codes listed below)

▶ 101 (salaried employment)

▶ 102 (daily/hourly wage job)

▶ 103 (piecework job)

▶ 104 (assistant to a family business)

▶ 105 (self-employment, no staff)

▶ 106 (self-employment, with staff)

Θ5) Expertise (indicate using one of the codes listed below)

▶ 201 (manager, executive)

▶ 202 (researcher, academic, artist)

▶ 203 (technologist, technical assistant)

▶ 204 (office clerk/employee)

▶ 205 (employed in services sector, retail and open markets)

▶ 206 (farmer, stock breeder, forester, fisherman)

▶ 207 (skilled technician)

▶ 208 (operator of industrial machinery)
▶ 209 (unskilled worker, manual labourer, small entrepreneur)
Θ6) Industry
▶ 301 (agriculture, live stock farm, hunting, forestry)
▶ 302 (fishing)
▶ 303 (mine, stone-pit, quarry)
▶ 304 (processing/manufacturing)
▶ 305 (utilities - electric power, natural gas, water)
▶ 306 (sales, repairs)
▶ 307 (hotels, restaurants)
▶ 308 (transports, storage, communications)
▶ 309 (real estate)
▶ 310 (banking, insurance, stock market, brokerage services etc)
▶ 311 (education)
▶ 312 (health and social welfare)
▶ 313 (services)
▶ 314 (domestic worker)
▶ 315 (construction)
Section I
I1) Indicate annual net income from employment activity in Greece
I2) Mark X in the box if you receive a pension
I3) If applicable, indicate the type of pension (issuing body)
I4) Mark X in the box if you receive an allowance/benefits
I5) If applicable, indicate the type of allowance/benefits (issuing body)
I6) Indicate the number of dependants living with you in Greece
Section IA
IA1) Illiterate: Mark X in the appropriate box (Yes/No)
IA2) Completed primary school: (Yes/No)
IA3) Completed middle school (Yes/No)
IA4) Completed secondary school (Yes/No)

IA5) University undergraduate (Yes/No)
IA6) University graduate (Yes/No)
Section IB
IB1) Indicate your native language (in Greek)
IB2) Indicate your religion
IB3) Indicate your ethnic origin, regardless of citizenship
IB4) Mark X in the appropriate box (Not at all / A little / So-so
/ Well / Very well) for the following statements:
‣ I can speak Greek
‣ I can read Greek
‣ I can write Greek

Greek citizenship through naturalisation

Acquiring citizenship through naturalisation is a long, expensive and complicated process. Applications take several years to be reviewed and many are rejected.

To be eligible for citizenship through naturalisation, foreigners (both EU and non-EU citizens) must be over 18 and not have a criminal record or a deportation order issued against them.

Applicants also have to fulfil certain statutory conditions, including having a total of 10 years' residency in Greece in the 12 years preceding the date of the application. Refugees (those who are recognised under the 1951 Geneva Convention on Refugees) should have a total of five years' residency.

The only exception to the residency requirement concerns foreigners who were born and raised in Greece. They may apply on their 18th birthday.

Foreigners married to Greeks have to prove at least three years of continuous residence. This 36-month countdown begins from the day of the wedding. The couple must also have a child together, or else the non-Greek spouse has to reside in Greece for ten years.

The second main condition to acquiring citizenship through naturalisation is a Greek language requirement. Applicants must be fluent in Greek.

The procedure

The application for Greek citizenship through naturalisation is submitted to the applicant's local municipality or village council. It must be accompanied by the following documents.

▶ A statement of naturalisation signed in the presence of the mayor or the head of the village council and two witnesses (Greek citizens)

▶ A photocopy of the applicant's passport or valid travel document. A translation is required if the information on this document is not written in Latin characters

▶ A photocopy of the applicant's residence permit

▶ A photocopy of the applicant's birth certificate. Note: This is not required for refugees

▶ A photocopy of the applicant's most recent income tax return

▶ Applicants must also have their fingerprints taken at their local police station and include verification with their application

▶ A non-refundable processing fee (1,470 euros) must be paid at the time of the application

The application and all the required documents are examined by the local prefecture. If prefecture officials find all the requirements in order, the application is forwarded to the regional general secretary for approval.

If this application is approved, officials at the regional office request a copy of the applicant's Type A criminal record certificate from the justice ministry. The application is then forwarded to the interior ministry, where officials request a personal interview with the applicant to determine his/her proficiency level in the Greek language, character and personality. If the applicant does not show up at this interview, his/her request for citizenship is automatically rejected.

If the application for citizenship is rejected, the foreigner may apply again after one year. The fee to do so is 734 euros.

If an application is approved, this decision is published in the *Government Gazette*.

The next step is for the applicant to take an oath. It is only after one takes this oath that they become Greek citizens. The oath must be taken within one year of the date the decision is published in the *Government Gazette*.

The oath: "I swear to be true to my homeland, to obey the constitution and the laws of this country and to consciously fulfil my duties as a Greek citizen."

People of Greek descent who live abroad
Non-nationals of Greek descent who reside abroad may also acquire Greek citizenship. They must submit an application to their local Greek consular office. Here are the application requirements.

▶ A statement of naturalisation signed in the presence of the consul and two Greek citizens, who serve as witnesses

▶ A certified photocopy of his/her passport or valid travel document. A translation is also required if the information on this document is not in Latin letters

▶ His/her birth certificate

▶ A Type A criminal record certificate

The application is forwarded to the Greek interior ministry, where officials review it and render a decision.

Info box

▶ Interior ministry's citizens' information 1564

▶ Interior ministry's citizenship office, tel 210-324-9314

▶ Foreign ministry's citizens' information office, 3 Akadimias St, tel 210-368-2700

Voting rights

European Union citizens who reside in Greece and are over the age of 18 may vote and stand in municipal elections. All they have to do is register at their local municipality and have their names included on the electoral roll.

EU Directive 94/80/EC grants citizens of any EU member state the right to vote and stand as a candidate in local elections in the member state in which they reside. The same conditions that apply to nationals of the country also apply to EU citizens. This directive was passed into Greek law in 1996.

Non-Greek EU citizens were first granted the right to vote in Greece's municipal elections by a 1997 presidential decree. The decree, however, does not establish their right to be elected as mayors or heads of municipal councils. For more information about EU citizens' right to vote and stand in municipal elections ring the interior ministry's election office (2 Evangelistrias St, Mitropoleos Square) on 210-322-3736.

Greek general elections

Only Greek citizens who are at least 18 years old may vote. Voting is compulsory for all Greeks over 18. To find out where you vote, ring the interior ministry's citizen information hotline (1564) or check online (*www.ypes.g*), *or contact your local municipality. Polling stations are usually set up at schools and other public buildings.*

If your name appears in two or more lists, you must vote in the municipality where you were last registered. You will be asked to sign a sworn statement at the polling station stating you are aware that you are listed more than once but that you will vote only once. This will be cross-checked by interior ministry officials. Voting more than once is prohibited and punishable by up to one year in prison.

Greek passports

Local prefectures stopped issuing passports in January 2006. In response to growing concerns about national and global security, the production and issuing of passports was assigned to the public order ministry. New passport offices have been set up in more than 100 police stations nationwide. Offices also opened at Greek consulates and embassies abroad. To find the nearest one, ring the OTE directory information 11888.

The new biometric passports are produced at a new central office in the eastern Athens suburb of Kessariani (8 Hiou St). The multimillion-euro technology necessary to mass-produce the new passports was purchased from TOPPAN, a Japanese company. The same printing technology is currently being used for passport production in countries like the United States, Canada and New Zealand.

Only the new biometric passports are accepted as of 1 January 2007. The new documents are harder to forge. Access to the high-security Kessariani office is off-limits to the general public. The new digitised passport fulfils a European Council regulation approved in December 2004. The directive mandates the inclusion of a facial image and fingerprints in passports issued by all 25 European Union member states. The regulation is aimed at protecting passports against falsification and at harmonising security features used in the production of the documents.

In compliance with recommendations of the International Civil Aviation Organisation (ICAO), the new passports include an embedded 'contactless' radio chip that stores the biometric identifiers (digitised fingerprints and a face scan).

The applicant must submit his/her application in person. There are five application requirements:

1) Application form (available at all application centres)
2) A recent digitised photograph

3) A photocopy of both sides of your Greek identification card

4) A statutory declaration (*ypefthini dilosi*) stating whether you have ever been convicted of forgery or making a false statement regarding the issuing of a passport and whether you are currently facing criminal charges. The statutory declaration must also indicate whether you have evaded the mandatory draft (for adult males) and whether the courts have denied you the right to leave the country

5) A receipt of payment for the following fees: 26.00 euros for a standard passport valid for five years and an additional 45 euros for the passport booklet, plus an additional 5 euro additional fee. TOTAL: 76.00 euros. Children pay the 45.00 + 5.00 euro fees, plus an additional 4.80 euros for each year that the passport is valid. These fees are paid at the tax office or at a Citizens' Service Centre (KEP).

The photograph

The photograph must be taken by a commercial photographer. It has to meet several specifications. For instance, it must have been taken within the last 12 months. The size of the photo must be 40mm wide and 60mm long and must be printed on high-quality photographic paper. Photos must be taken with uniform lighting so as not to show shadows or backgrounds. Photos must show the full front view of the face, centred in the photo and squared to the camera. Eyes must be open and clearly visible. Glasses may be worn, but the eyes must be visible. Sunglasses are not acceptable. Hats are not permitted. Religious head coverings may be worn, provided that the full facial features are clearly visible. Facial expression must be neutral (no smiling or frowning) with the mouth closed. Red eyes are not acceptable.

The new adult passports are valid for five years. The ones issued to children under age 14 are valid for two years. Passports issued to children over age 14 are valid until their 18th birthday.

Foreign driving permits

Driving licences issued by European Union member states are recognised in Greece.

Permits from Canada, Australia, Japan and the United States can be converted to Greek ones without a driving test. The main criterion for the conversion of licences issued in these four countries is that the permit be valid at the time the application is submitted. The following documents are also required:

▶ An official translation (issued by the foreign ministry or a certified lawyer) of the foreign driver's licence

▶ The actual driver's licence

▶ A photocopy of the applicant's residence permit, or identification card if the applicant is a Greek citizen. Note: the residence permit must be issued at least six months before

▶ 1 colour passport-size photograph

▶ A receipt from the National Bank of Greece stating that 64 euros has been deposited in the "special account of ND 538/70" at the National Bank of Greece

▶ A receipt from the tax office that you have paid an 18 euro processing fee for the licence

▶ Health certificates from a pathologist and an optometrist

These documents should be submitted to your local prefecture's transportation office (*diefthinsi metaforon*).

It takes several days for the application to be processed. The Greek permit expires on the applicant's 65th birthday. For more information ring your local prefecture's transportation office (*diefthinsi metaforon*).

Greek driving permits

Is a Greek driver's licence the only thing keeping you from the open road? You'll have to pass the Greek driving test. You must be at least 18 years old. Here's how to do it.

▶ Sign up for driving lessons. You are required to take at least 20 hours of theory lessons and another 20 hours of practical driving lessons. The written test is based on a book of 1,100 driving-related questions.

▶ Once you have completed the required number of lessons, you need to go to your nearest local transport ministry office to submit a driving test application. You also need to submit a statutory declaration stating your name and address. Greek citizens must present ID cards, and foreigners must show residence permits. (Note: Residence permits should have been issued at least 185 days before driving test applications are submitted.)

▶ Applications should be accompanied by a certificate issued by a pathologist and a certificate that an optometrist has tested your eyesight.

▶ You need to produce two National Bank of Greece receipts, each for 48 euros (96 euros total). You also need two receipts issued by the tax office. One that you have paid 6 euros and the other for 18 euros

▶ Once you have submitted your application, you have to sign up for the written test. The test is in Greek. There is no charge. Candidates are required to answer 30 questions, making no more than one mistake.

Foreigners who are not fluent in Greek can ask to have a foreign ministry translator with them during the test. It costs about 100 euros to hire a translator. He/she reads the test questions out loud.

▶ The driving test is next. It costs about 200 euros. The examiner evaluates the candidate's knowledge about what is under the vehicle's bonnet (engine etc, as well as how well they parallel park, reverse on a turn, brake suddenly, change gears at the top of a hill and make a three-point turn). Those who pass the test will be issued a licence that expires on their 65th birthday. The licence can be renewed almost automatically. The holder simply has to pass a health examination and an eye-test.

If you fail the written test (answer more than one question wrong) you will have to take six more theory lessons. If you fail a second time, you are required to take another three lessons. Should you fail the driving test, you will have to take 10 more practical lessons before retaking the test.

New EU rules on the road

A single credit card-sized driving licence will replace some 110 different versions currently in use across the European Union, under new rules approved by the European Parliament.

More than 200 million Europeans who currently hold licences for cars, motorcycles, buses, vans and trucks will be able obtain the new licence, which will be valid for up to 15 years. Permits for trucks and buses will be valid for five years.

There will be a graded licensing system for motorcycle riders who are more likely to be involved in accidents. New motorcyclists will be required to gain experience on smaller motorcycles before moving to more powerful bikes.

Governments will start issuing the EU licence in 2012 and have until 2032 to phase out current permits.

Renting a home

A re you looking for a new apartment or house to rent? Before you make a move, make sure you know your renter's rights and responsibilities.

Tenants do have rights, as well as duties. A few points you should keep in mind.

The lease is a written agreement between the tenant and the landlord. Before you sign on the dotted line, read the contract carefully. Discuss anything you do not understand with your landlord. The lease should state the following:

▶ The names of the landlord and tenant as well as a description of the apartment or house.

▶ The amount of rent the tenant must pay and when it is due, as well as the amount of the security deposit, if one is requested by the landlord.

▶ A security deposit (one- or two-month rent) is returned to the tenant when the lease is up if there are no outstanding bills or damages to the apartment or house. Note: A security deposit is not required by Greek law. Most landlords also require tenants to pay the first and last month's rent upon moving in.

▶ The term of the lease (two-year lease, three etc) and options for what happens at the end of this period (renew the lease, increase rent etc).

▶ Always keep a copy of the lease in a safe place.

▶ Also ask about the payment of the duty stamp (*hartosimo*), which is added on top of the rent. This is about 5 percent of a month's rent. Usually, the tenant pays half.

▶ By law, the term of the lease should be for at least three years. Even if the lease expires in less than three years, the landlord cannot evict the tenant until the full three years are up.

▶ It is also common practice for the tenant to pay the municipal rates charged through the electricity (DEI) bill. However, this is meant to be paid by the owners.

▶ By law, the tenant cannot leave before the lease expires. If this does happen, the landlord has the right to sue the tenant, which is rare. It is common practice for the tenant to give the landlord at least one month's notice. In the worst-case scenario, the landlord keeps the security deposit.

▶ Rent increases: These are usually specified in the lease. Most landlords request a 10 percent rental increase upon renewal of the lease. However, if this is not specified, the increase is only 75 percent of the cost of living index.

▶ Think twice about signing a lease that states that all damages must be repaired by the tenant. Under Greek law, a fresh coat of paint, a leaky tap and other damages caused by normal daily use are the landlord's responsibility. But if the lease states otherwise, the written agreement supersedes the law.

▶ It is a good idea to inspect the condition of the apartment or house with the landlord and make an inventory of any damages before you move in. This should be dated and signed by both you and your landlord. This way you will not have to pay for damages caused by previous tenants.

▶ Always keep the receipts when you pay the rent.

▶ If you do not pay your rent, the owner can legally evict you. The procedure takes about three to four months.

For more information about renters' rights and obligations contact the Panhellenic Renters' Protection Association. Its office is located at 66 Menandrou St, Omonia, tel 210-524-6982.

Buying a home

Whether you are Greek or German, British or Bulgarian, buying a property in Greece begins with a dream. The dream is like a film played in fast forward. It starts with the desire to own a home, continues rapidly with the viewing process when you fall in love with the perfect residence and then skips forward to the moving in and cocktails on the balcony while you watch the sun dip into the Aegean - or some such romantic vision.

All well and good, but the practicalities of buying a home in Greece mean that between the viewing and the celebratory cocktails there is a maze of red tape that, at best, will take the sheen off the glazed cherry and, at worst, scupper the entire transaction.

In many aspects of life, Greece can be a bureaucratic nightmare but, contrary to popular belief, the buying system is not the maze of thorns and dead ends that most people expect. Certain elements of the buying process here are a marked improvement on similar systems elsewhere.

For example, the purchaser is protected against "gazumping", the underhand system in England where the vendor can sell to another buyer at any stage of the process until contracts are exchanged - even when he/she has already accepted an offer.

So how do you get the process moving?

Lawyer

The key to a comfortable passage is a good, independent lawyer who will be thorough in chasing up the paperwork and in protecting you every step of the way. If you do not speak Greek then it is important that you have someone who speaks your language. Reassurance is vital, especially if you are conducting the transaction from any distance.

How do you find a good lawyer? Many people already have

a "family" lawyer who will be able to recommend someone well-versed in property law. If you don't have one of these, then the agent who is selling the property will usually recommend a few lawyers in the area.

Some people might raise their eyebrows about using an agent's choice of lawyer, but usually they will only recommend them because they have found them to be competent in the past. Any doubts and you can ask for recommendations. If they give you a list of people who have bought property using their services make sure you call two or three of them to find out about their experiences.

In order to avoid endless trips to offices it's a good idea to make the lawyer your proxy. He will then sign documents on your behalf, which is another good reason to have one who speaks your language.

Tax number

To buy a property in Greece you will need a tax number (the AFM). Citizens and residents will already have this, but foreigners will need to register. This should be the first job that your lawyer does. If the property is being bought jointly each of the purchasers will need his or her own tax number.

Finance

Although you will only hand over the final payment at the end of the procedure when you sign the contracts, it is important to make sure that the money is in position as early as possible (and that you know what budget you are working within). Usually you will need a deposit of around ten percent once your offer has been accepted. There are also taxes and fees to bear in mind (*see below*).

Many people deal in cash. This is the simplest form of transaction and has remained popular because for many years

Greek banks have been so backward in offering mortgages. Now the banks are getting their act together, so getting a mortgage is becoming more common. The purchaser will need proof of employment or income. If self-employed they will need to see previous tax returns.

If the purchaser is a non-Greek, then the bank may still require a Greek guarantor. But if you are looking to use a Greek bank, again you should start the process early.

Deposit

Once the purchasers have had an offer accepted they will need to pay a deposit - usually around ten percent. At this point a pre-contract agreement is drawn up by the lawyers, which will prevent the vendor from dealing with another agent or selling to another purchaser.

If the searches expose information not previously known (for example that it's an illegal building) then the purchaser can withdraw from the sale and get the deposit back. If, however, he pulls out for no reasonable cause then he loses the deposit.

On the other hand, if the vendor pulls out without reasonable cause, he is liable to repay to the purchaser the deposit (or double in some cases).

Paperwork

One of the things you will pay your lawyer for is the gathering together of all the relevant paperwork. You need four items:

▶ The deeds of ownership: an obvious and straightforward requirement establishing that the vendor is indeed the owner of the property.

▶ A topographical plan: an important safeguard for the boundaries of the property. Your lawyer will get a surveyor to do this properly.

▶ A planning permit: this is to make sure that the house you are buying is actually legal.

▶ A Forestry Commission certificate: if you are looking to buy a property outside the local building zone you will need this to confirm that the plot you are intending to buy is not considered forestry.

If there are no problems with the paperwork, the whole of this process should take between a fortnight and a month. Occasionally, however, there may be a delay on a piece of paperwork.

Possible complications

▶ Multiple owners: usually this is not a problem, as multiple owners will normally appoint one or two of their number to act for all of them. If one of the owners starts to cause problems, it is probably wise to walk away from the deal.

▶ Outstanding debt on the property: this can cause delays but need not be terminal if arrangements are made by the vendor to pay money to the bank at the same time as the contracts for the property are signed. The purchaser will need to trust the judgement of his lawyer.

▶ Tax clearance: the vendor needs a tax clearance form from the tax office to show that he does not owe tax to the state, as well as an E9 form to prove he has declared his property.

▶ Irregularities on planning permits and topographical plans: in the past, planning laws have been routinely ignored with owners building a house of, say, 120 square metres when they only have permission to build 100 square metres. This makes the property illegal. In order to proceed with the sale, the owner will need to legalise his building by applying for planning permission and paying the penalty incurred. The legalisation process takes about three or four months. Sometimes a building can't be legalised because, for example, it may have been built too close to a neighbouring building or because it has been built higher than the local authority permits. In these cases consult your lawyer.

▶ Ownership disputes: because there is no complete land registry, there can be disputes about who actually owns the land, especially as squatting for 20 years effectively gives the squatter the right to ownership. Sometimes when properties have been handed down through families for generations, no deeds actually exist. In this case the vendor needs to legalise his ownership with the public notary through a *xrisiktisia* (a document signed by him and witnessed by neighbours to prove that he really does own the property).

▶ An *aera*: This usually occurs in towns and cities when the vendor sells the building rights to the possible floors above you: this point of law is a personal choice for the purchaser.

Signing contracts

The contract is drawn up by the public notary. It will usually be signed by the lawyers for each party at the notary's office. The notary will witness the contract.

The purchaser can attend and sign if he wishes. If he is a non-Greek he is obliged to have the contract read to him in his own tongue by an interpreter which his lawyer will arrange. For a fee of between 80 and 200 euros he can also have it translated.

The original is kept at the public notary's office, a second is sent to the registry office and the purchaser takes a third copy.

Tax

The purchaser is liable to pay purchase tax on the property he buys. As per applicable law, in the areas where there exists a fire department, the tax rate is set at nine percent for a value of up to 15,000 euros and at 11 percent for values above this amount. The lawyer should inform you at the start of the process what the figure will be.

This may depend on a number of things. If you are a Greek first-time buyer then the property is effectively tax-free because of the allowances permitted. This can also vary depending on family circumstances.

The tax you pay will also depend on whether the purchase price in the contract is entered as the actual price (the amount of cash that changes hands) or the taxable price (the amount that the local authority says it is worth).

There can be a major difference between these two prices which must both be entered on the contract. It has become standard practice to enter the taxable price as the actual price: whether this is tax avoidance or tax evasion is a grey area in the law and purchasers who want to enter the lower price may find that their lawyer declines to sign the contract on their behalf. In which case, they have to sign themselves.

The government recently announced that VAT would be applied to newly built properties from 1 January 2006. Other tax changes are in the air, so purchasers are advised to clarify the tax situation with their lawyer as early as possible in the process as it will considerably affect the final financial outlay.

There is no Capital Gains Tax in Greece at the moment, so profit made on the property stays with the vendor.

Other costs

Apart from paying tax on the property, the purchaser will also face a number of other costs in completing the deal. These are:

▶ Lawyer: around 1,500-2,000 euros
▶ Surveyor: around 500 euros
▶ Public notary: around two percent of the purchase price
▶ Lawyers' Association: 1 percent of first 44,000 euros and 0.5 percent of the remainder of the purchase price (eg on a property whose purchase price is 100,000 euros, the fee will be 440 euros plus 280 euros - a total of 720 euros)

(Compiled by Barney Spender with the help of Mary O'Connor, a partner in O'Connor Properties in the Peloponnese, www.oconnorproperties.gr)

Greek language certificate

*M*ilate *Ellinika? Nai?* Prove it. Immigrants, repatriated Greeks and all learners of Modern Greek abroad can obtain official documentation of their competency level by sitting an examination offered by the Greek Language Centre.

Candidates are examined in four different levels of linguistic proficiency: reading comprehension, writing, verbal comprehension and speaking. The examinations are open to everyone over the age of 12. Those who make the grade are awarded an official certificate of attainment in Greek, which is issued by the education ministry.

In Greece, examinations are held at the Greek Language Centre in Thessaloniki and at the Hellenic American Union (HAU) in downtown Athens.

What are the four levels?

▶ Holders of a Level A certificate are capable of communicating orally in daily situations, can understand basic announcements on the radio and television and have basic reading and writing skills.

▶ Holders of a Level B certificate can easily comprehend oral and written instructions, and can express their ideas both verbally and on paper.

▶ Holders of Level C have enough knowledge of the Greek language to articulately express their ideas and views in a formal and informal setting.

▶ Holders of Level D possess the language skills required in the professional world.

Where do these certificates come in handy?

These certificates offer learners an expert and objective opinion of the level of their knowledge and comprehension of the Greek language. Until recently, there was no official certification available for immigrants and repatriated Greeks, as well as Greeks abroad and those who spoke the language to some degree. Only those who studied Modern Greek in university possessed widely recognised certification.

This all changed in 1999, when the Centre for Greek Language began to administer these examinations in Europe, and in 2000 in Greece and worldwide.

Today, these certificates are a basic professional and academic requirement. For instance, based on a 1999 presidential decree (138/9-7-99) immigrants who have not graduated from a Greek high school are required to hold a Level C certificate in order to attend a Greek university and other public institutions of higher learning. The Level D certificate allows non-Greek EU citizens to apply for employment in the Greek public sector. Employers in the private sector also require a level of proficiency in the language, and the certificates serve as official proof of linguistic proficiency.

Level A and B certificates are also recommended as preparation for the tests at higher levels.

Are candidates required to pass all levels?

No. A candidate who is fluent in Greek may take the examination for Level C or D without holding the junior levels (A and B). They also do not have to prove that they have taken Greek-language lessons.

When is registration?

The examinations in Greece and abroad are held mid-May each year. Registration begins in February. For more information in Greece contact the Greek Language Centre in Thessaloniki or Greek embassies abroad.

How much does it cost?

Prices are subject to change annually. Level A and B exams cost about 65 euros and Levels C and D are at 75 euros.

For more information contact the Greek Language Centre in Thessaloniki located at 17 Karamaouna St, Skra Square, tel 2310 459101. Send an email to *antonopoulou@greeklanguage. gr* or visit the website *www.greeklanguage.gr*

Translating official documents

The foreign ministry's translation office is located at 10 Arionos St in Psyrri. Offices on the first floor assist those seeking to translate documents from Albanian, Bulgarian, Georgian, Croatian, Moldovan, Ukrainian, Uzbek, Hungarian, Polish, Romanian, Russian, Serbian, Slovakian and Czech into Greek and vice versa. The entire second floor caters to those wishing to translate documents from English into Greek and vice versa.

The third-floor offices handle translations from Arabic, French, German, Spanish, Italian, Dutch, Portuguese, Swedish, Turkish and Finnish into Greek and vice versa. The department that certifies documents is also on the third floor.

The office is open to the public on weekdays between 8.30am and 1pm.

The procedure

Step 1: Make sure you have with you the original document or a certified photocopy. Documents issued abroad must be certified by the embassy. Documents issued in Greece can be certified at your local police station or at one of the interior ministry's Citizens' Information Centres - *Kentro Enimerosis Politon* - (call 1564 for details).

Step 2: Fill in an application form available at the translation office. The application is in Greek, English, Russian and Albanian. You are required to indicate the language of the document, the language of the translation, the applicant's name and telephone number, as well as the number of your Greek identification card or passport.

Step 3: Submit all documents. Employees will issue a protocol number which indicates the date you should return to pick up the translation. Do not lose this slip.

Step 4: Pay the full price of the translation or a deposit upon submission and the rest when you pick up the translation.

Translation fee

Different fees apply for different documents to be translated. A birth certificate costs about 7 euros (issued in six working days) or about 10 euros (issued in three working days). A university diploma costs about 8 euros (issued in five days) or about 12 euros (issued in three days).

People who do not live in Athens may mail the document they wish to have translated to the translation office. In this case they must pay by a postal cheque *(tahydromiki epitagi)*. For more information, contact the translation office on 210-328-5713.

The Greek tax roll number (AFM)

Dying to pay taxes? Before you even begin to think about it, get an AFM (ΑΦΜ).

An AFM is a tax roll number. Everyone in Greece who works or owns property, a car, a boat etc - and thus has to file tax declarations - needs one of these numbers. To get this nine-digit number you have to submit an application at your local tax office. It is a relatively painless procedure. Here's how to apply for an AFM.

▶ Go to your local tax office. Greeks who reside abroad but wish to obtain an AFM should go to the expatriates' tax office in Athens at 4 Metsovou St (tel 210-820-4652)

▶ You will be asked to file an M1 form. It's a standard form: name, address, telephone number etc.

▶ If you are a Greek citizen, you need to show your ID card and submit a photocopy of this card.

▶ EU citizens will need to show either their passport or ID card. Non-EU foreigners need to present their passport or another valid travel document and their residence permit. Certified photocopies of both documents must be submitted. Note: Applicants must also obtain a translation of their passport or other travel document only if the information is not in Latin characters. The document can either be translated by the foreign ministry or a certified lawyer. A birth certificate may also be required if an applicant's passport does not indicate mother's full name.

▶ The tax office employee will then process the information on a computer. This should only take a few minutes. A printout with the AFM number is issued.

Why do you need an AFM?

▶ To work in Greece

▶ To buy or rent a home

▶ To buy a car, truck, motorcycle, boat, aeroplane, helicopter and, if you wish, to get a licence to drive, sail or fly one of these vehicles

The Citizens' Service Centre (KEP)

D on't waste time shuttling between government agencies to get your paperwork done. Head to your nearest Citizens' Service Centre (KEP).

These free-of-charge centres are devoted to making the often arduous, time-consuming process of obtaining government documents a little bit easier. They are designed to take on the bureaucratic legwork for you.

How it works

One needs only to call the service line number 1564 (there are also foreign-language speakers on staff) to see if the Citizens' Service Centre can assist with the paperwork needed. You can either schedule an appointment through 1564, or simply show up at the centre. A staff member will take on your case, either providing paperwork from online services, or filling out the appropriate electronic application.

The staff member contacts the appropriate government service(s) and in a matter of days, weeks or months, acquires the necessary paperwork. The client either returns to the centre to pick up the documents, or goes to another agency or government organisation to receive the needed paperwork. The citizens' service centres are opened 8am-8pm Monday-Friday and Saturday 8am-2pm.

Over the telephone

Ring 1502 (8am-8pm Monday-Friday) to apply for government documents. Each call costs 2.20 euros. Greek citizens must have their ID card number and immigrants their residence card number at hand when calling. Over 150 different types of government documents can be requested over the telephone. The documents available range from a photocopy of one's university degree (only for those who have graduated from a Greek state university) and certification of one's business licence to certificates stating one is a pensioner and documents verifying that they are insured, as well as Greek passports.

The ombudsman

The office of the Greek ombudsman deals with citizen grievances against public agencies and bureaucracy. This non-judicial mechanism for the resolution of differences between citizen and state opened its doors in October 1998. The office received some 7,300 complaints during its first year of operation. This is a record number of complaints for the European Union. France's ombudsman, for instance, received only some 6,000 complaints during its first three years.

The lion's share of grievances each year is against social insurance foundations, such as IKA, and local government, namely municipalities and prefectures. Below is how you can ask the ombudsman to help resolve your complaint when hampered by maladministration at public offices and state agencies.

▶ Write a letter of complaint. This should include personal details (name, address, telephone number) and a brief outline of the facts and other important details relevant to the complaint. The letter should be dated and signed by the complainant.

▶ The letter can be submitted to the ombudsman's office in person. The office is open to the public 8.30am-2pm, Monday to Friday. Or you can send a fax to 210-729-2129. Or send a letter by mail to 5 Hadziyanni-Mexis St, Athens TK 11528.

▶ The complaint should be lodged within 6 months of the event that prompted it.

▶ The ombudsman's office will send a letter to the complainant to inform if it is accepting the case. If so, the complainant will be provided with the contact information from the person who will be investigating the matter.

▶ Each complaint submitted to the ombudsman is reviewed by deputy ombudsmen in one of the five departments: human rights (deals with cases involving individual, political or social rights); health and social welfare (deals with cases involving social insurance, health, public health care, welfare of elderly, children, jobless and people with special needs); quality of life (cases involving land use, urban planning, public works, culture and the environment); state-citizen relations (general issues of maladministration and lack of adherence to legal principles); and children's rights.

The ombudsman may request public sector services to provide him with any information, document or other evidence relating to the case and may examine individuals, perform an on-the-spot examination and order an expert's report. All documents must be made available, unless they involve national defence and state security confidentiality. The refusal of a public functionary or civil servant or member of the administration to cooperate with the ombudsman during an investigation constitutes a disciplinary offence of breach of duty and a reason for their replacement.

Senior and junior investigators for the ombudsman also provide information on various matters including how the office operates. They also direct people to the appropriate government agencies in cases that fall outside the ombudsman's jurisdiction. No appointment is necessary. The public reception office is open Monday to Friday 8.30am to 2pm.

For information ring 210 728 9600 or 801 112 5000

The European Union ombudsman

M istreated or cheated by a European Union body? Turn to the European ombudsman, whose job is to look into complaints of maladministration by institutions and bodies within the European Union. Institutions and bodies that come under the European ombudsman's jurisdiction are the European Commission, Council of the European Union, European Parliament, Court of Auditors, Court of Justice (apart from its judicial role), Economic and Social Committee, Committee of the Regions, European Central Bank and European Investment Bank.

The European ombudsman does not accept complaints concerning national, regional or local administrations of the 27 EU member states. These should be registered with the national ombudsman.

The European ombudsman accepts complaints about poor management in the activities of the above mentioned institutions and bodies of the European Union. These activities include instances of administrative indiscretion, unfairness, discrimination, abuse of power, lack of - or refusal to provide - information, and unjustified delay. The European ombudsman will not deal with any cases set to go to court or that have been settled by a court.

Many of the complaints made to date concern administrative delay, lack of transparency or refusal of access to information. A number of complaints concern work relations and the recruitment of staff.

To make a complaint to the European ombudsman, write a letter in any of the official EU languages clearly stating who you are, which institution or body of the European Union you are complaining about and the grounds for your complaint. The complaint must be filed within 24 months after the incident. Before turning to the European ombudsman, make sure you've contacted - in the form of a letter - the institution or body concerned. Send letters by post, e-mail or fax.

The office of the European ombudsman is located at 1 Avenue du President Robert Schuman, Strasbourg. For info ring +33 (0) 3 88 17 23 13, fax 33 (0) 3 88 17 90 62 or e-mail *euro-ombudsman@europarl.eu. int*

Complain to the European Commission

Anyone (EU citizen or a resident in an EU country) may lodge a complaint with the European Commission against a member state about any measure (law, regulation or administrative action) which they consider incompatible with a provision or principle of EU law. A letter of complaint may be mailed to the following address:

Commission of the European Communities
(Attn: Secretary-General)
B-1049 Brussels
BELGIUM

A letter of complaint may also be delivered to the European Commission's representative office in Athens (2 Vas Sofias Ave, tel 210-727-2100)

The banking ombudsman

Make your moan count. If you have a problem with your bank and can't seem to resolve the dispute, turn to the Greek banking ombudsman. Thousands have taken their grievances to this institution and many of them have found solutions.

The banking ombudsman examines complaints related to banking services, everything from savings accounts and loans to cheques and credit cards. As in other countries, the ombudsman is an independent institution aimed at resolving disputes in a fair, impartial and transparent manner.

The main cause of disputes between clients and their banks is that the former are generally not sufficiently informed about the terms under which the banks provide services and products. Bank employees do not always take the time to explain the fine print or provide enough advice and direction.

How to complain

Step one: Take up your complaint with the person in charge at your local bank, eg department supervisor or branch manager. They should be able to provide you with a response or a solution within 10 working days.

Step two: If there is no response or you are unsatisfied with the solution suggested, contact your bank's customer service department. They too should provide you with a written response within 10 working days.

Step three: If they do not respond or you are still not satisfied, file a complaint with the banking ombudsman. You must do so within one month from the bank's response or the end of the 10-day time limit.

The banking ombudsman accepts only written complaints. Forms (in Greek and English) are available at all bank branches across the country. The form must be completed and the dispute clearly described in a few paragraphs. The originals or certified photocopies of all relevant documents must also be submitted. This complaint form can be mailed or personally delivered to the banking ombudsman's office at 12-14 Karagiorgi Servias St, Athens. The applicant is promptly informed, in writing, of receipt of the complaint.

Examining grievances

All complaints are examined "quickly and confidentially". The banking ombudsman cannot examine complaints that have not been taken up with the bank manager or the customer service department. The ombudsman will also not review grievances if more than a month has passed since the bank's customer service department's response. And the ombudsman will not interfere in matters that are pending before the court.

For more information on Greece's banking ombudsman call 210-337-6700, email *contact@bank-omb. gr* or log onto *www. bank-omb.gr*.

Solvit: the EU trouble-shooter

Having a hard time getting your professional qualifications recognised in another European Union country? Need advice about living, working or retiring in the EU? Answers to all these questions and more are just a phone call away. The European Commission's Citizens Signpost Service (dial 00-800-67891011 - the same number applies throughout the EU) answers your questions and helps you overcome any hurdles you encounter along the way.

And to make things even easier, the European Commission has set up a new problem-solving network called Solvit, which handles complaints involving the misapplication of EU legislation. All EU citizens and businesses can contact Solvit centres directly by calling the number above.

These services are part of the EU's Europe Direct programme, which started as a pilot project in 1996. EU citizens can seek free advice and problem-solving services in any of the official EU languages. Questions are answered within three working days or less by an EU law expert. Answers include clear and concise explanations of EU legislation relating to the problem and advice on where the citizen can go for further information and assistance (at European, national, regional or local levels). The Signpost Service also follows up with further guidance if the citizen has additional questions or finds discrepancies between theory and practice.

The Solvit service deals with cases of misapplication of EU law by public authorities in each of the EU member states. EU citizens and businesses can call on this service to solve cross-border problems and intervene in instances where they feel their rights are being violated.

Signpost services in practice

The Citizens Signpost Service can work to help people get the information and advice they need. Below are a few examples.

▶ After moving to a different member state, you've been trying for some time without success to get a job in your own profession but haven't been able to get your qualifications recognised in the new country of residence. The Signpost Service can tell you exactly what your rights are and who to contact to make sure those rights are enforced.

▶ You feel you have a better chance of finding work in another EU country. Will you be eligible for unemployment benefits in that country while looking for work? Will you need a residence permit? The Signpost Service can answer these questions based on your personal situation. And if you find that the host member state is not enforcing the rules, you can contact the service again for advice on what to do. Legal experts may refer you to a local Solvit centre, which can work on your behalf with the responsible authorities.

▶ After living and working elsewhere in the EU for a number of years, you wish to return to your country of origin to work and later retire there. You've accumulated many years of pension contributions during your time abroad and have no longer been paying contributions in your home country. Is there a European Union system to facilitate transferring pension rights back to the country you plan to retire in?

▶ A family moves to another EU country for 10 years. The wife works while the husband looks after the children. During their stay, the wife spends two years working back in her country of origin, but the rest of the family does not follow her there. A couple of years later, the host authorities ask the family to pay back two years of the social security allowances they have been receiving for the dependent children on the grounds that the breadwinner was not working in the country during that period. The wife contacts the authorities in the country where she had been working for those two years and they tell her she is not eligible to receive allowances there either. Where, if anywhere, is the family entitled to receive the allowance over the period concerned? Do they have to reimburse the money they have received?

There are Solvit centres set up in each of the member states. In Greece, this centre is located at 5 Nikis St, Syntagma Square (at the finance ministry). For more information, ring 210-333-2462 or email *markt@mnec.gr*

Consumer rights

The customer is always right, so they say. But what happens if a consumer believes he or she has been ripped off, bamboozled, scammed or swindled? File a complaint. The government council for consumer rights (KEPKE) is on your side. The council is made up of nine consumer group representatives, two consumer rights experts, nine representatives of the General Confederation of Workers in Greece (GSEE) and over a dozen representatives of the various trade unions.

KEPKE is the state's committee on consumer policy, which is headed by the development ministry's office of the general secretariat for consumers. This office is aimed at safeguarding consumers' rights. It informs citizens of their rights, investigates complaints lodged by consumers and imposes penalties upon private and public companies and agencies. Consumers who wish to learn more about their rights or would like to file a complaint can telephone KEPKE on 1520 (weekdays 8am-10pm and weekends between 8am and 3pm). By ringing this toll-free hotline number, consumers can request information or file a complaint about faulty or defective products; inaccurate, misleading or deceiving advertisements; below-standard services and other instances of profiteering and exploitation.

The information from KEPKE is available only in Greek. You can also file a complaint online by visiting *www.efpolis.gr*

The European Consumer Centre:

Athens' European Consumer Centre is aimed at helping consumers exercise their rights when shopping in another member state. Citizens are urged to learn about their rights when buying goods or services across borders within the EU's internal market. The Athens centre's job is to help Greek consumers enjoy the full benefits of the EU's internal market. It is part of the so-called Euroguichet network of consumer advice offices across Europe.

ATHENS NEWS

The Athens office is hosted by the Greek Consumer Institute (INKA) and jointly funded by the European Commission, the Central Bank of Greece and the development ministry. Information is available in both Greek and English.

The centre is also open to EU citizens visiting Greece who feel they have been swindled, ripped off or bamboozled, and to people living in Greece who feel they have been scammed by businesses in other EU member states. The most common complaints involving purchases concern overpricing, faulty or defective products, inaccurate, misleading or deceiving advertisements and below-standard services as well as instances of exploitation.

Poor-quality services include food, public transport and taxis. Another frequent gripe involves instances where consumers have not received products they have purchased through the mail from other EU countries. Europeans vacationing in Greece often complain about travel and accommodation services that are not up to par.

The European Consumer Centre is open to all consumers, not only to investigate complaints but also to provide people with information about their rights as consumers in Greece and in the European Union. If a consumer lives in Greece and has a dispute with a retailer or business in another European country, they may seek assistance at the centre. If the consumer lives in another member state and has a dispute with a retailer in Greece, they may seek retribution through the European Consumer Centre in their home country.

However, if a consumer living in Greece has a complaint against a Greek retailer, they should ring INKA on 210-363-2443 or 6945-888409 (emergencies only) or fax 210-363-3976. Information is also available online (*www. inka.gr*), while a new website will soon provide information about consumer rights in Europe. The European Consumer Centre is located in downtown Athens at 7 Akadimias St (8th floor).

Disgruntled consumers in Greece may also turn to Consumer Organisation EKPIZO. The group's head office is located at 43-45 Valtetsiou St in Athens. For more information ring 210-330-4444.

Tourist police

To serve and protect: The tourist police are accessible 24 hours a day, seven days a week. Just call 171. The Greek National Tourist Organisation (EOT) encourages foreign tourists visiting Greece to call this three-digit helpline for information on a range of services. Information is available in Greek, English, Italian, French and German.

Operators can inform tourists about public transport and domestic ferry and airline schedules, as well as their rights. By calling 171, Greek and foreign visitors can also lodge complaints about hotels, restaurants, taxis and other services. The tourist police are responsible for handling these complaints and investigating any problems visitors to Greece have experienced. Tourists are especially vulnerable to profiteering and poor-quality service. Many incidents reported are in connection with consumers' issues including everything from inflated taxi fares to late departures.

Transporting a dead body overseas

The death of a loved one is a difficult experience, made more complicated by the many arrangements that must be made.

In the case of tourists and immigrants who die in Greece, their next of kin must make the necessary preparations to send the body home. Here are the requirements and the process for transporting the deceased abroad.

▶ Death certificate

▶ Certificate of embalming issued by a local morgue, which states that the body has been embalmed for transportation overseas

▶ The certificate of embalming is submitted to the local health board

▶ The local prefecture office must be notified about the plans to transport the body overseas. The prefecture officials will then call a doctor who seals the casket. The sealing is undertaken in the presence of three witnesses - officials from the national narcotics, currency fraud and trafficking task forces (to ensure that there is indeed a corpse and only a corpse in the casket)

▶ The death certificate, the embalming certificate and a certificate issued by the local customs authorities in accordance with the regulations for transporting a corpse overseas must be translated into the official language of the destination country. The translations can be made by embassy officials or at the foreign ministry

▶ All the translated documents are then taken to the airline company or the shipping company (depending on how the corpse will be transported). The casket is weighed by the company to determine the cost of transport

▶ The consul of the destination country must also be notified. Consul officials should issue a shipping permit. The required documents include a statement as to the identity of the deceased, burial permit and a permit to transport the remains issued by local authorities, a certified copy of the death certificate, a certificate issued by local medical authorities that the death was not the result of a contagious disease and that the body has been prepared and placed in a casket as required by the medical authorities, and that no hazard to health is created by shipping the remains

Note: The body must be placed in a special wooden, metal-lined, air-tight casket, which in turn is placed in a standard wooden shipping box.

▶ The cost to transport a body overseas ranges between 1,500 euros and as much as 4,000 euros (depending on the destination and the type of casket the next of kin selects)

▶ The procedure to transport a body overseas is undertaken by funeral parlours. But not all funeral parlours perform this service. There are about two dozen in Athens and Thessaloniki and several on some of the larger islands like Crete and Corfu. To find the nearest funeral parlour, check your local advertising directory (yellow pages)

Filling in tax forms

Those of you who have had the pleasure of a longtime acquaintance with the Greek tax system surely remember a not-so-distant time when filing meant interminable lines at a local tax office or a post office, usually on the last possible deadline.

Nowadays, with the option of filing your income statements electronically, things have improved a bit. But, even for the simplest cases - a wage earner, for example, with no other sources of income - the forms remain quite complex, and you still have to be aware of your specific deadline among the multiple deadlines for filing income statements.

We have compiled a simple guide that will help you avoid some basic mistakes. We have focused on wage earners, who are more than 90 percent of foreigners declaring taxes in Greece. We will, however, touch upon matters that concern self-employed professionals (who must file their own returns), for instance, because many employees have another job on the side and must also file the form relevant to such activities. We will explain these different tax forms in detail, especially the main form (E1), the professionals' form (E3) and the property form (E9).

In this section, we will deal with the basic things: who must file an income declaration form, when and how. We will also deal with some basic issues, such as the income tax bands and any changes in tax legislation that affect this year's declarations.

Who must file an income declaration form?

- Those whose earned 2007 income exceeds 3,000 euros (6,000 euros for salaried employees if their salary is their unique income source).
- Those, independent of income, who acquired a property (by selling another, taking a loan, or through inheritance).
- Car owners whose already declared car was bought after 1 January 1993 and its discounted worth is equal to, or

exceeds, 50,000 euros.

- Owners of any kind of boat over 10m long (or smaller if you employed a crew during the year), or aircraft, or a truck, including Jeeps, but excluding farmers' trucks.
- All self-employed professionals or company owners (in total or partly).
- Anyone with an income from rents exceeding 600 euros.
- Anyone who began building a house within the last year or who bought property, cars, leisure boats or aircraft.
- Everyone living in a house (owned, not rented) exceeding 200 square metres.
- Anyone owning a secondary residence (or more), with a total area exceeding 150 sqm.
- Farmers with an income lower than 3,000 euros but who have received subsidies in excess of 1,500 euros for plant products or 2,250 euros for animal products.
- Farmers taking loans (for professional purposes) with an outstanding amount exceeding 5,900 euros on 31 December 2007.
- Farmers cultivating products in greenhouses exceeding 2,000 sqm (2 stremmas, or half an acre).
- Those who sell farm or other products at flea markets or as itinerant sellers.
- Finally, all those not falling in the above categories but invited, in writing, by the head of the local tax office to file. That is, those suspected of cheating, at the tax authorities' discretion.

Remember, their attitude over all taxpayers is that they are potential dodgers. And, given the amount of tax dodging in Greece (studies estimate taxable, that is non-criminal, grey market activity at about 28 percent of the country's GDP), they are often right, even though you might find their treatment of you insulting. In their defence, their manners have improved over the years.

When do we have to file?

In contrast with the United States, for example, where there is a single deadline, there are numerous different deadlines, depending on the kind of economic activity you engage in. Since we are assuming you are wage earners, or pensioners, the following table concerns the deadlines applicable to you, according to your Tax Register Serial Number (ΑΦΜ - AFM).

AFM number ends in:	Filing deadline in 2007
1	May 3
2	May 7
3	May 9
4	May 11
5	May 15
6	May 17
7	May 21
8	May 23
9	May 25
10, 20, 30, 40, 50	May 30
60, 70, 80, 90, 00	June 1
No AFM	June 1

If you also earn income from other activities (professionals, company owners etc), even if these constitute the majority of your income, the above deadlines are valid, because they are the latest chronologically. That is, you are not required to submit income declaration forms at the same time, as say, professionals (who must submit theirs in the first half of March). But, it is advisable to file early, especially if you expect a reimbursement, as most wage earners normally do. You will get your money earlier. And, of course, do not file late. The fine is an additional 1 percent on your tax for every month you delay; or, if you are tax-exempt, you will be slapped a fine ranging from 117 euros to 1,170 euros.

How can we file the income declaration?

- To your local tax office, in duplicate. Keep an extra copy for your records. You can also do it by proxy.
- By registered mail, also in duplicate. The post office stamp is proof of the date of filing.
- Through a Citizens' Assistance Centre (KEP), either in duplicate, as you would through the tax office or the post, or online, through one of their computers, if available.
- Through an accountant, who can fill in your forms. You buy the accountant's expertise for a fee, which varies according to the complexity of the case.
- Through the Internet *(see below)*.

Should I file through the Internet?

If you have an online connection, filing through the Internet makes sense. Besides the obvious avoidance of queues, especially if you file at or near the deadline, you can file in your own time and place (that is, from anywhere in the world), it will be processed much earlier and, if you have to pay additional tax, you get a 1.5 percent discount (capped at 118 euros).

Also, if filing online, you can file the E9 form - the one detailing your property holdings - later (between June 10 and July 10, depending on your AΦM). If you follow the old paper route, you must submit this form along with the others.

A few days ago, the government decided to provide another incentive: those filing their income statements through the Internet have an additional 10 working days past the deadline provided for those who file them on paper, either at the tax authority offices or through the post. For example: if the deadline that applies to you is Wednesday, May 23, you can file online until just before the start of the working day on Thursday, June 7 (that is, at 7.59 am). Don't stretch it, though: the system is programmed not to accept any late filings and, being past the deadline for filing on paper, you will not avoid a fine if you go past that.

Drawbacks: The online page, accessible via *www.gsis.gr* or, more directly, through *www.taxisnet.gr*, is supposed to have an English version, which, at the time of this writing, is still "under development", that is, nonexistent. You are prompted to return to the Greek page. So, if you do not speak Greek, or feel comfortable enough to understand the forms, you are out of luck.

Early processing means early results. Which is fine, if tax is returned to you. In the opposite case, you have to pay your additional tax quicker. It's up to you to estimate whether it is preferable to file online or leave it to the overworked, and not exactly speedy anyway, local tax people to delay the processing.

How can I file online?

Go to *www.gsis.gr* or *www.taxisnet.gr* and register. You should do this at least a few days before the deadline because it usually takes up to 5 working days to receive your access code and password by email. Also, write your access code somewhere because it is an unwieldy thing - a combination of 12 digits and letters - which, unlike your password, you cannot change. Registering is free. Navigation is very easy and you do not need to change your code numbers every year.

Online filing is easy: the system is available on a 24-hour, 7-days-per-week basis. However, make sure to check your forms carefully before you hit the "send" button (Υποβολή Δήλωσης). You have the option to save your form(s) as a draft, in case you would like to inspect them again at a later time prior to sending them in. Not many of us are very comfortable working with online forms; the computer-savvy generation has not started paying taxes yet. So, be careful. If you feel more comfortable with pen and paper, go to the local tax office, get some forms and fill them in before filing electronically.

Remember, hitting "send" is an irrevocable act. Fortunately, the system scrutinises the sent form for any basic omission and warns you. Otherwise, it sends you a message, in Greek, that "Your Filing Was Successfully Completed on [date]" and gives you a protocol number, which may be of use in subsequent dealings with the tax office. You can print the electronic forms at home or from any printer connected to a computer with online access. The printouts are considered official documents.

If you have any problems with the system, you can call 210-480-2552 or email taxisnet@taxisnet.gr.

Important: When filing online, you do not have to send documents such as proofs of purchase, insurance or rent payments (on which you get tax breaks). But, you will have to keep those documents for five years, during which time the tax office can call on you anytime to produce them.

Tax rates for 2008

The major change for 2008 is in the income tax brackets. Apart from the 1,000 euro increase in tax-exempt income levels, the 15 percent band (up to 13,000 euros last year) is eliminated. The tax rate for income up to 30,000 euros is lowered to 29 percent and a new income band (30,000-75,000 euros) is introduced with a tax rate of 39 percent. Thus, the top tax rate of 40 percent now applies for incomes over 75,000 euros.

The following tables provide a reminder about the current income tax bands for wage earners and pensioners:

Number of children	Part of income (€)	Tax (%)	Tax (€)	Total income (€)	Total tax (€)
None	First 12,000	0	0	12,000	0
(or single)	Next 18,000	29	5,220	30,000	5,220
	Next 45,000	39	17,550	75,000	22,770
	Above that	40	*	*	*
One	First 13,000	0	0	13,000	0
	Next 17,000	29	4,930	30,000	4,930

	Next 45,000	39	17,550	75,000	22,480
	Above that	40	*	*	*
Two	First 14,000	0	0	14,000	0
	Next 16,000	29	4,640	30,000	4,640
	Next 45,000	39	17,550	75,000	22,190
	Above that	40	*	*	*
Three	First 22,000	0	0	22,000	0
	Next 8,000	29	2,320	30,000	2,320
	Next 45,000	39	17,550	75,000	19,870
	Above that	40	*	*	*

* Varies

For each additional child, the tax-exempt portion of income rises by 1,000 euros.

The tax rates for the income brackets up to 30,000 euros and between 30,000-75,000 euros will decrease to 27 and 37 percent, respectively, in 2009 (for 2008 incomes) and to 25 and 35 percent in 2010. The top rate for incomes exceeding 75,000 euros will remain at 40 percent.

NOTE 1: This is a provisional table because there is no way to know whether the government will increase tax breaks for big families or the poorest.

NOTE 2: This table concerns wage earners. For all other categories of income earners, the tax exempt portion of income is 10,500 euros, rising for people with children as in the table above.

Filling in the E1

The main income declaration form is the E1. We assume that you are in the vast majority of non-Greek tax declarants who are either salaried or pensioned, and may or may not have secondary income from other sources such as commercial activity or rent.

If you are single, the process is simpler (although you pay

higher taxes). If you are a married couple (married by December 31, 2007), the law requires that you file a single E1 form. The form is filed by the husband, but both have to sign it.

There are three exceptions: separation (you need to prove it), bankruptcy by either husband or wife and court-ordered incapacitation (for sentencing or other reasons). The tax is assessed separately in any of these cases.

Table 1: (Personal Data I)

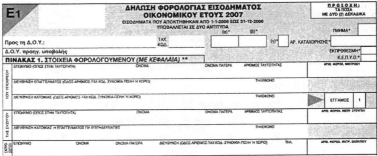

If you have filed income declarations before, you will get the E1 form in the mail. Otherwise, you can obtain it from your local tax office. In case you get it in the mail, you will find most of Table 1 already completed for you: surname, name, father's name, ID number, AΦM number, your workplace and home addresses. If any of this information needs to be changed, you can do so in the form. Do not be put off by tax office employees that say you must make a written declaration to the tax office's registry department: you can do that in the form itself.

If you file your declaration through a representative, Table 1 provides space to list his/her name, father's name, address, telephone and AΦM number.

Foreign citizens who have not filed before need to get an AΦM (tax registry number). You can get one by going to the tax office with your passport and, if you reside in Greece, your residence permit. If your passport is not written in Latin characters, you must submit a photocopy of the original, along with an official translation.

Table 2: (Personal Data II)

ΠΙΝΑΚΑΣ 2. ΠΛΗΡΟΦΟΡΙΑΚΑ ΣΤΟΙΧΕΙΑ (συμπληρώνονται μόνο σε καταφατική περίπτωση)	Υπόχρεου			Της συζύγου		
1. Είστε νέος φορολογούμενος (υποβάλλετε δήλωση για πρώτη φορά);	327 ΝΑΙ 1			328 ΝΑΙ 1		
2. Είστε κάτοικος εξωτερικού και αποκτάτε εισόδημα στην Ελλάδα;	319 ΝΑΙ 1			320 ΝΑΙ 1		
3. Υποβάλλεται η δήλωση από κηδεμόνα σχολάζουσας κληρονομιάς, μεσεγγυούχο ή προσωρινό διαχειριστή;	329 ΝΑΙ 1					
4. Υποβάλλεται η δήλωση από επίτροπο, κηδεμόνα ανηλίκου ή δικαστικό συμπαραστάτη;	330 ΝΑΙ 1					
5. Υποβάλλεται η δήλωση από κληρονόμο του φορολογουμένου που απεβίωσε;	331 ΝΑΙ 1					
6. Είστε συνταξιούχος και γεννηθήκατε πριν από το 1942;	013 ΝΑΙ 1			014 ΝΑΙ 1		
7. Είστε μισθωτός ή συνταξιούχος και εργασθήκατε ή κατοικήσατε μέσα στο 2006 σε παραμεθόρια περιοχή;	015 ΝΑΙ 1			016 ΝΑΙ 1		
8. Οι εκπτώσεις και μειώσεις των Πινάκων 3 και 7 να γίνουν από τα ποσά των κωδικών 307 ή 308 (βουλευτές - δικαστές);	309 ΝΑΙ 1	ΟΧΙ 2	310 ΝΑΙ 1		ΟΧΙ 2	
9. Είστε μισθωτός και πήρατε στεγαστικό επίδομα μέσα στο 2006;	011 ΝΑΙ 1			012 ΝΑΙ 1		
10. Κατοικείτε μόνιμα σε νησί με πληθυσμό κάτω από 3.100 κατοίκους;	007 ΝΑΙ 1			008 ΝΑΙ 1		
11. Ασκείτε ατομική εμπορική επιχ/ση σε οικισμό κάτω των 1.000 κατοίκων;***	017 ΝΑΙ 1			018 ΝΑΙ 1		
12. Μεταβλήθηκε η περιουσιακή σας κατάσταση ή άλλα στοιχεία του Ε9 το 2006;	617 ΝΑΙ 1					
13. Είστε κάτοικος χώρας της Ε.Ε. (εκτός Ελλάδας) και αποκτήσατε στην Ελλάδα πάνω από το 90% του συνολικού εισοδήματός σας;	385 ΝΑΙ 1			386 ΝΑΙ 1		
14. Ανήκετε στην κατηγορία των ολικώς τυφλών, παραπληγικών πάνω από 80% κτλ.;	905 ΝΑΙ 1			906 ΝΑΙ 1		
15. Είστε αξιωματικός ή ημεδαπό κατώτερο πλήρωμα εμπορικού πλοίου ή ιπτάμενο προσωπικό πολιτικής αεροπορίας;	911 ΝΑΙ 1			912 ΝΑΙ 1		

This table asks you a series of questions to determine whether you must file any exemptions from the norm as defined by the tax law. If any of these apply to you, you must mark the box saying NAI (yes) with an X.

The questions are:

1. Are you a new taxpayer (submitting a declaration for the first time)?

2. Is your main residence abroad and you earn income in Greece? [You must answer affirmatively even if you do not earn any income but either: a) own an expensive Greek-registered car (or yacht or aircraft) that is deemed a proof of high income b) own a residence c) are building one.]

3. Is the declaration submitted by: a trustee, depository or temporary administrator of an estate in abeyance [without a claimant]?

4. Is it submitted by a minor's legal guardian?

5. Is it submitted by an heir to a deceased taxpayer?

6. Are you a retiree born before 1942? [You may need to submit or show proof of this]

7. Are you a salaried pension and pensioner who worked or resided in a border region in 2007? [Border regions are the Xanthi, Rodopi, Evros, Lesvos, Chios, Samos, the Dodecanese prefectures and the areas of the Thesprotia, Ioannina, Kastoria, Florina, Pella, Kilkis, Serres and Drama prefectures located within 20 kilometres of the border. You need an affidavit by a mayor or other public authority as proof of residence plus a statement by your employer attesting to the time you spent there in 2007].

8. (This question applies to ministers, members of parliament and justices, active or retired, who get their own tax breaks.)

9. Are you a salaried employee and were you awarded a housing subsidy in 2007?

10. Are you a permanent resident of an island with fewer than 3,100 inhabitants? [You need a mayor's affidavit as proof of residence.]

11. Do you own an enterprise or are self-employed in a settlement with fewer than 1,000 residents? [The settlement must also not be considered as a tourist area.]

12. Did the state of your property holdings or other E9 data change during 2007? [Those who answer yes must also submit an E9 form.]

13. Are you a resident of a European Union member country (other than Greece) who earned over 90% of your total income in Greece?

14. Are you among the 100% blind or those with over 80% disability etc.?

15. Are you an armed forces officer or member of the crew in a merchant ship [non-officer] or airline?

Table 3: (Disability tax breaks)

ΠΙΝΑΚΑΣ 3. ΑΦΑΙΡΕΣΗ ΠΟΣΟΥ ΛΟΓΩ ΑΝΑΠΗΡΙΑΣ κτλ. ΚΑΙ ΜΕΙΩΣΗ ΦΟΡΟΥ				
1. Εχετε δικαίωμα έκπτωσης ποσού 1.900 ευρώ λόγω αναπηρίας 67% και πάνω κτλ.;	001	NAI 1	002	NAI 1
2. Αριθμός παιδιών του Πίνακα 9 περίπτ. 1 (αριθμητικά)	003		004	
3. Αριθμός προσώπων του Πίνακα 9 με αναπηρία 67% και πάνω κτλ. (αριθμητικά)	005		006	

Asks whether you (3.1) or any family members (3.2-3.3) are eligible for a tax break due to severe disability. You must submit, together with the E1 form, a copy of a decision by a medical committee attesting that you or a family member is disabled.

Depending on the type of disability, this decision is either temporary or permanent. In the latter case, you only need to submit it once, when it is issued. Blind people need an affidavit by the prefecture that they are enrolled in a special register kept for the blind in each prefecture.

Table 4: Income subject to tax (and sources of income)

4A: Salaried services

ΠΙΝΑΚΑΣ 4. ΦΟΡΟΛΟΓΟΥΜΕΝΑ ΕΙΣΟΔΗΜΑΤΑ		
Α. ΕΙΣΟΔΗΜΑ ΑΠΟ ΜΙΣΘΩΤΕΣ ΥΠΗΡΕΣΙΕΣ		
1. Άθροισμα καθαρών ποσών από μισθούς, ημερομίσθια κτλ. (εκτός περιπτ. 2, 3, 4, 5 και 6)	301	302
2. Άθροισμα καθαρών ποσών από κύριες συντάξεις (εκτός περιπτ. 1, 3, 4, 5, και 6)	303	304
3. Άθροισμα καθαρών ποσών από επικουρικές συντάξεις, μερίσματα, κτλ. (εκτός περιπτ. 1, 2, 4, 5 και 6)	321	322
4. Καθαρό ποσό επιδόματος κοινωνικής αλληλεγγύης (ΕΚΑΣ)	305	306
5. Αμοιβές γιατρών του ΕΣΥ κτλ. (εφημερίες), αθλητών που θέλετε να φορολογηθείτε με τις γενικές διατάξεις	317	318
6. Άθροισμα καθαρών εισοδημάτων που φορολογούνται με το Ζ ψήφισμα (βουλευτές-δικαστές)	307	308

Here you enter net income earned from wages (boxes 301-302), main pensions (303-304), auxiliary pension funds (321-322) and the state bonus given to low-income pensioners (305-306). There are also special categories for doctors' payments for being on duty in National Health Service hospitals, professional athletes and subsidies for parents of three or more children (317-318) and for members of parliament, ministers and judges (307-308).

Taxable salaried income includes not just salaries but also any bonuses you get from your employer, including subsidised rents, company cars and even hired help for the home. It does not include travelling expenses or the lump sum payment made to several employees, especially civil servants, upon retirement. Also exempt from tax is any bonus paid as part of a voluntary early retirement scheme.

Your employer must provide you with a slip detailing your salary, taxes and social security contributions paid in advance by February 15. Like all other supporting documents, you do not submit it when filing online but must keep it for five years in case the tax authorities decide to do a backdated check of your income declarations.

Farmers' pensions are included here, not in table 4B.

4B: Farming

B. ΕΙΣΟΔΗΜΑ ΑΠΟ ΓΕΩΡΓΙΚΕΣ ΕΠΙΧΕΙΡΗΣΕΙΣ						
1. Καθαρό εισόδημα ατομικής επιχείρησης με βάση τα βιβλία ή στοιχεία				461		462
2. Καθαρό εισόδημα ατομικής επιχείρησης με βάση το αντικειμενικό σύστημα						
Νομός (Δήμος/Διαμέρισμα ή Κοινότητα) ονοματεπώνυμο/Επωνυμία	Είδος παραγωγής α) είδος καλλιέργειας, στ) β) είδος κτήματος, ζ) γ) είδος, είδος, μονάδες	Αριθμός (1) στρεμμάτων Η (Αριθ. τ/ άλλων μονάδων)	Έδαφος Ημερινό Πεδινό	Αρδευόμενο Μη αρδευόμενο	Καθαρό εισόδημα (2) ανα στρέμμα ή ανα κεφαλή ζώου ή ανά άλλη μονάδα	Συνολικό Καθαρό Εισόδημα (3) = (1) x (2)
Σύνολο καθαρού γεωργικού εισοδήματος με βάση το αντικειμενικό σύστημα				915		916

			Υπόχρεου		Της συζύγου
Μείον: α) Ενοίκια που καταβλήθηκαν για μίσθωση γεωργικής γης			335		336
β) Αξία καινούργιου πάγιου εξοπλισμού 326 , x 25% ή 50%			337		338
γ) Για κατά κύριο επάγγελμα αγρότες 1.500 ή 3.000 ευρώ αν πήραν εξισωτικές αποζημιώσεις					
ή 2.250(ή 1.875) ή 4.500 (ή 3.750) ευρώ, αντίστοιχα, αν είναι νέοι αγρότες			339		340
3. Ζημιά του ίδιου οικονομικού έτους από ατομική άσκηση γεωργικής επιχείρησης			465		466
4. Ζημιές προηγούμενων οικονομικών ετών από ατομική άσκηση γεωργικής επιχείρησης			467		468
5. Ακαθάριστα έσοδα από ατομική άσκηση νεωργικής επιχείρησης			475		476

Farmers are those earning at least 50 percent of their total income from farming activities. If you happen to be among the minority that own a farming enterprise that keeps books, then you fill boxes 461-462. If not, your taxable income is calculated using so-called objective criteria. The first column is the location of the farm, the second describes the kind of farming activity (cultivation, livestock) you engage in, the third is the cultivated area (in stremmas: 1 stremma is 1,000 square metres, or about a fourth of an acre and a tenth of a hectare) and/or number of animals, the fourth column asks you to describe the kind of terrain (mountainous, semi-mountainous, plain), in the fifth you must specify whether your farmland is irrigated or not. The sixth column asks for your net income per stremma or per animal: this you will complete using the "objective criteria" tables compiled by the ministry of finance and available at local authorities, farm cooperatives or tax offices.

Finally, you declare your total net income by multiplying your per unit income by the number of units (stremmas or animals) that you own (boxes 915-916).

From that income you deduct rents paid for land (boxes 335-336). You need either a copy of the contract, the rent payment receipts or a certified affidavit that you pay this rent.

Box 326 asks for the value of fixed equipment acquired in

2007 (you need the receipts and an affidavit stating the equipment will be used exclusively for farming activities) and in boxes 337-338 you write the tax-deductible portion of the equipment's value (25 percent or 50 percent if you are a "young farmer", that is, under 40 years old).

You are also asked to declare any losses from farming activities from previous years which you can transfer to 2007 (boxes 467-468) and your gross earnings in 2007 (475-476).

4C: Commercial activities

Γ. ΕΙΣΟΔΗΜΑ ΑΠΟ ΕΜΠΟΡΙΚΕΣ ΕΠΙΧΕΙΡΗΣΕΙΣ		
1. Καθαρά κέρδη από ατομική επιχείρηση (εκτός περίπτ. 4)	401	402
2. Επιχειρηματική αμοιβή από Ο.Ε. ή Ε.Ε. ή κοινωνία κληρονομικού δικαίου	403	404
3. Καθαρά κέρδη από Ο.Ε. ή Ε.Ε. ή Κοινωνία κτλ. μη υπαγόμενες στο άρθρο 10 Κ.Φ.Ε.	405	406
4. Υπερτίμημα από πώληση αυτοκινήτου επιχείρησης	407	408
5. Ζημιά του ίδιου οικονομικού έτους από ατομική επιχείρηση (εκτός περίπτ. 4)	413	414
6. Ζημιές προηγούμενων οικονομικών ετών από ατομική επιχείρηση	415	416
7. Ακαθάριστα έσοδα από ατομική επιχείρηση	425	426

For reasons of space, we have decided not to cover such activities, but only self-employed professionals.

1. Net profit from a commercial enterprise (except case 4). (Boxes 401-402.) In order to fill this, you must fill the E3 form first.

2. Corporate fees from ordinary partnership (OE) or limited partnership (EE) companies.

3. Net profits from an OE or EE company or a corporation not included under Article 10 of the Tax Code. This obscure language refers to companies owning up to two vehicles for professional uses (taxes, buses, trucks).

4. Added value from selling a company vehicle.

5. Losses incurred in 2007 (except under case 4).

6. Losses incurred in previous years that can be transferred into 2007.

7. Turnover from an individual enterprise (not a partnership or corporation).

4D: Self-employment

There are complicated rules as to who is considered a self-employed professional, but those of you who have already braved the bureaucratic hurdles to declare yourselves as such know who you are. Thus, there is no need to duplicate here the long list of professions and services under this category.

Δ. ΕΙΣΟΔΗΜΑ ΑΠΟ ΕΛΕΥΘΕΡΙΑ ΕΠΑΓΓΕΛΜΑΤΑ		
1. Καθαρό εισόδημα από ατομικό επάγγελμα	501	502
2. Ποσό διατροφής που έχει εισπραχθεί από σύζυγο (εκτός των παιδιών)	505	506
3. Εισόδημα που δεν εντάσσεται σε άλλη περίπτ. του Πίν. 4	507	508
4. Ζημιά του ίδιου οικονομικού έτους από ατομικό επάγγελμα	511	512
5. Ακαθάριστα έσοδα από ατομική άσκηση ελευθέριου επαγγέλματος	517	518

As for those engaged in commercial activity, you should first fill in the E3 form. Self-employed professionals should really look only at Tables A, B, E, ΣΤ, Z and I (see below for details).

1. You declare your net income as a self-employed professional in boxes 501-502.

2. Since the tax authorities bundle under this category all sources of income not otherwise classified, if you are divorced you declare the alimony you received from your ex-husband or –wife in 2007. You need to submit an affidavit declaring the income received plus a copy of the court decision or agreement through a notary of the alimony paid. Alimony received directly by children is not included. The person who pays the alimony declares the expense in Table 7 (boxes 075-076).

3. Here you declare income not declared in any other section of Table 4. One example is income you derive by leasing a movable property (eg a car).

4. If you have incurred losses and you have decided against following the self-audit procedure, you declare your losses in boxes 511-512. If you do use self-audit (more on this in the E3 section), do not fill the boxes.

5. You fill in the gross earnings from your activity in boxes 517-518. This exempts earnings from activity abroad.

4E: Property

Anyone with income from property rentals must also submit the E2 form. You submit only one copy of this form. If both the husband and wife derive income from rents, they submit separate E2 forms, not one form as in the case of E1.

Ε. ΕΙΣΟΔΗΜΑ ΑΠΟ ΑΚΙΝΗΤΑ	1. Ακαθάριστο εισόδημα από εκμίσθωση:				
α) κατοικιών, ξενοδοχείων, κλινικών, σχολείων, αιθουσών κιν/φων ή θεάτρων κτλ.		103		104	
β) καταστημάτων, γραφείων, αποθηκών κτλ.		105		106	
γ) γηπέδων, χώρων τοποθέτησης επιγραφών κτλ.		107		108	
δ) βιομηχανοστασίων		109		110	
ε) γαιών		101		102	
στ) γαιών με βάση το αντικειμενικό σύστημα		909		910	
2. α) Ακαθάριστο εισόδημα από υπεκμίσθωση ακινήτων		111		112	
β) Στην περίπτωση αυτή, ποιο μίσθωμα έχετε καταβάλει		113		114	
3. Ακαθάριστο εισόδημα από δωρεάν παραχώρηση - ιδιόχρηση:					
α) κατοικιών (μόνο δωρεάν παραχώρηση)		129		130	
β) σχολείων, ξενοδοχείων, κλινικών, αιθουσών κινηματογράφων ή θεάτρων κτλ.		143		144	
γ) καταστημάτων, γραφείων, αποθηκών κτλ.		145		146	
δ) γηπέδων		147		148	
ε) γαιών (μόνο δωρεάν παραχώρηση)		141		142	
στ) γαιών (μόνο δωρεάν παραχώρηση) με βάση το αντικειμενικό σύστημα		701		702	
4. Δαπάνες κτλ. για: α) κατοικίες, ξενοδοχεία κτλ. (περιπτ. 1α, 3α, 3β)		151		152	
β) καταστήματα, γραφεία κτλ. (περιπτ. 1β, 1δ, 3γ)		157		158	
5. α) Αποζημίωση που καταβλήθηκε με βάση νόμο στο μισθωτή ακινήτου όταν λυθεί επαγγελματική μίσθωση		163		164	
β) Ακαθάριστο εισόδημα από την εκμίσθωση του ακινήτου της περιπτ. 5α		165		166	
6. Λοιπές περιπτ. Άρθρου 23 Κ.Φ.Ε. (γαίες κτλ.)		159		160	
7. Ακαθάριστο εισόδημα των περιπτ. 1α, 2α και 3α από κατοικίες με επιφάνεια πάνω από από 300 τ.μ. η καθεμιά		175		176	
8. Ακαθάριστο εισόδημα των περιπτ. 1α, 3α και 3β που έχουν χαρακτηριστεί διατηρητέες		177		178	
9. Ακαθάριστο εισόδημα των περ.1β,1δ και 3γ που έχουν χαρακτηριστεί διατηρητέες		179		180	
10. Δαπάνες για διατηρητέα ακίνητα των περιπτ. 8 και 9		181		182	
11. Ακαθάριστο εισόδημα (από επίταξη ακινήτων, κτλ.) για το οποίο δε βεβαιώνεται τέλος χαρτοσήμου		741		742	

1. In this section you declare your gross income from renting property. This property is divided into:

a) Residences, hotels, hospitals, schools, cinemas and theatres (boxes 103-104).

b) Shops, offices, warehouses (105-106).

c) Sports grounds (or courts), space for advertisements and any income derived from the building on property you own by someone who rents the property (107-108).

d) Factories (109-110).

e) Farms or land plots (101-102).

f) Land plots taxed according to the "objective value" system (909-910). You fill this in only if the rent you declare in boxes 101-102 is less than the one estimated using the "objective value" system.

2. If you sublet property you have rented, you declare your income in boxes 111-112. You also declare the rent you pay yourself in 113-114.

3. This section concerns property (divided into the same categories as in section 1) that you have actually permitted others to use for free or you are using yourself (the latter only in cases

3b, 3c and 3d). Here, you do not declare any actual income, but the imputed rent you would have earned, based on the property's size and use. A notable exception: if you have let your children or parents use a residence you own for free, you only declare the imputed rent for the area in excess of 200 square metres.

4. Any expenses you have incurred for your properties (insurance against fire and other risks, repairs and maintenance, lawyers' fees in case of disputes with the tenants) you write either in boxes 151-152 (for property under sections 1a, 3a and 3b) or 157-158 (for property under sections 1b, 1d, 3c). You need to submit supporting documents for these expenses. In the case of insurance, the contract must specify the insured property's location (address and floor if part of an apartment building); otherwise, you need a separate affidavit from the insurer.

5. In case you terminate a business property rental contract early and compensate the tenant, you declare the compensation amount in boxes 163-164. You also declare your gross income from this particular property in boxes 165-166.

6. Other expenditures, such as any state taxes on land plots, is registered in boxes 159-160.

7. In case you own a residence with an area of more than 300 square metres, you declare your gross income in boxes 175-176 (you pay additional tax for it).

8. In case any of your properties falling under sections 1a, 3a and 3b are listed, you declare the income derived from them in boxes 177-178.

9. Same for properties listed under sections 1b, 1d and 3c (179-180)

10. You declare expenses made for the above listed properties in 181-182.

11. Income from requisition of properties (for which you pay no stamp duty) is declared in 741-742.

4F: Movables

ΣΤ. ΕΙΣΟΔΗΜΑ ΑΠΟ ΚΙΝΗΤΕΣ ΑΞΙΕΣ
Καθαρό εισόδημα από τόκους δανείων κτλ. ημεδαπής προέλευσης ____ 291 ____ 292

Here you declare any income from interest, dividends and the like from domestic sources only. You do not declare income from: dividends from corporations, interest earned on treasury bills and bonds and interest on savings. On the other hand, you declare interest from corporate bonds.

4G: Income earned abroad

Ζ. ΕΙΣΟΔΗΜΑ ΑΛΛΟΔΑΠΗΣ ΠΡΟΕΛΕΥΣΗΣ
1. Καθαρό ποσό από μισθούς, συντάξεις, κτλ. αλλοδαπής προέλευσης ____ 389 ____ 390
2. Καθαρά κέρδη από γεωργικές επιχειρήσεις (ατομική, εταιρικές) στην αλλοδαπή ____ 463 ____ 464
3. Ζημιές από γεωργικές επιχειρήσεις (ατομική, εταιρικές) στην αλλοδαπή ____ 471 ____ 472
4. Καθαρά κέρδη από εμπορικές επιχειρήσεις (ατομική, εταιρικές) στην αλλοδαπή ____ 411 ____ 412
5. Ζημιές από εμπορικές επιχειρήσεις (ατομική, εταιρικές) στην αλλοδαπή ____ 421 ____ 422
6. Καθαρά κέρδη από ελευθέριο επάγγελμα (ατομικά, εταιρικά) στην αλλοδαπή ____ 509 ____ 510
7. Ζημιές από ελευθέριο επάγγελμα (ατομικά, εταιρικά) στην αλλοδαπή ____ 513 ____ 514
8. Τόκοι και μερίσματα τίτλων κτλ. αλλοδαπής προέλευσης ____ 295 ____ 296
9. Τόκοι κτλ. αλλοδαπής προέλευσης υπαγόμενοι στην παρακράτηση του άρθ.10 του ν.3312/05 ____ 397 ____ 398
10. Ακαθάριστο εισόδημα από ακίνητα που βρίσκονται στην αλλοδαπή ____ 171 ____ 172
11. Καθαρό εισόδημα της περίπτ.10 ____ 173 ____ 174
12. Ακαθάριστο εισόδημα της περίπτ.10 από κατοικίες με επιφάνεια πάνω από 300 τ.μ. η καθεμιά ____ 395 ____ 396

If you reside in Greece, you must pay taxes for income earned abroad, irrespective of whether you are a Greek citizen or not. You are exempt from taxes only if your country of citizenship has signed a bilateral accord on avoidance of double taxation. Countries that have not signed such accords are Australia and Canada.

In Table 4G's sections, you declare the following:

1. Income earned in the form of salaries and pensions (boxes 389-390).

2. Net income from farming activity, either as a private individual or partner/shareholder in an enterprise (463-464). In case you are a partner or shareholder, you must submit an affidavit listing the company's name, its legal status, total net income and the stake you own in the company (this also holds for cases 3-7 below).

3. Losses from activities in the agricultural sector (471-472).

4. Net income from commercial activities (411-412).

5. Losses from commercial activities (421-422).

Surviving Greek Bureaucracy

6. Net income as a self-employed professional (509-510).

7. Losses as a self-employed professional (513-514).

8. Interest earned on savings, repos, bonds (295-296).

9. Same as in (8) in countries that have chosen to impose taxes themselves rather than disclose individuals' holdings. These are: Austria, Belgium, Luxembourg, San Marino, Andorra, Switzerland, Lichtenstein, Monaco, British Virgin Islands, the Isle of Man, the Channel Islands (Guernsey, Jersey), the Dutch Antilles and the Turks and Caicos islands (397-398).

10. Gross income from properties (171-172).

11. Net income from properties (173-174). You compute it by deducting expenses. You need documentation for non-recurring expenses.

12. Gross income from residences exceeding 300 square metres.

Table 5: Computation of imputed income

The tax authorities cannot possibly audit every taxpayer to find precisely which income to tax.

That is why the tax authorities invented the notion of imputed income. In simple terms, they say that a taxpayer who has bought certain items or lives a certain lifestyle must have a minimum income level, independently of what he or she declares.

To take one example only, the tax authorities have decided that, if your residence includes an indoor swimming pool larger than 120 square metres, the minimum level of living expenses cannot have been less than 70,200 euros, irrespective of when the house and the pool were built. That is then listed as your minimum allowable imputed income.

If you own an outdoor pool of the same size, the minimum imputed living expenses drop to 46,800 euros. So, if your declared income is 20% lower than this amount, the tax authority will simply disregard it and tax you for the imputed amount.

The imputed income sources are divided into two categories: ownership of certain luxury items (big cars and jeep-type vehicles, yachts and other leisure craft longer than 10 metres, employment of crew members on these craft, airplanes, helicopters, main residence over 200 square metres, secondary residences over 150 square metres, pools) and documented expenditure for the acquisition of certain types of property (including all the above-mentioned items) such as residences (over 120 square metres for a main residence), the building of such residences, property leasing or time-sharing, cars and motorcycles independent of size and any movable property worth over 5,000 euros (except for equipment for professional use).

Other sources of imputed income are donations and gifts over 300 euros (even to one's children but excluding donations and gifts to the state and local authorities), loans to individuals and payment of interest and/or principal for housing loans and non-consumer items. The tax authorities have strange views of what a "non-consumer item" is: among them, they include cars, motorcycles, paintings and any movable property worth over 5,000 euros.

Some items do not constitute sources of imputed income: they include all cars acquired before January 1, 1993, most cars acquired before January 1, 2004 and cars acquired after that and worth less than 50,000 euros.

Also, cars acquired by people with disabilities, cars acquired abroad and brought to Greece upon the owner's relocation (these are exempt for a period of two years) and any leisure craft acquired by people with a permanent residence abroad.

With these in mind, you may complete Table 5.

1. Section 1 asks for details of everything you have declared so far.

a) Annual imputed income for owned or rented main residence, and up to two secondary residences.

Residences run across the page, with the main residence topmost, followed by a non-vacation secondary residence and finally by a vacation secondary residence.

As you move across the page, a series of questions is asked for all three residences, creating columns of stacked boxes. In the first set of boxes, you are asked to declare location, including the streets around the city block where it is located.

You are asked to check the boxes numbered 206, 208, 210 if one of the properties has been inherited or gifted (from parents to children and vice versa).

Check boxes 203, 207, 209 if a property is rented.

The next set of unnumbered boxes asks if a property is an apartment or a stand-alone house, and the following one what floor it is on.

Check box 204 or 205 if one of your secondary residences is located in a place with fewer than 5,000 inhabitants.

Boxes 211, 218 and 225 ask for the floor space of each residence, and the following column (boxes 212, 219 and 226) for the square metreage of the garage or storage space.

The following two columns ask for the ownership percentage of each spouse, declarant (213, 220, 227) and wife (214, 221, 228).

The next column (215, 222, 229) asks for the number of months you have been inhabiting the residence(s).

The penultimate column asks for the objective values, or minimum prices of the residences (above 200 square metres for the main residence and 150 square metres for the secondary ones) and the final column asks for the year the building permit was issued or last revised.

b) If you have any other secondary residences, you record their annual imputed income in boxes 707-708.

c) You list the annual imputed expenditure for cars falling under the imputed income rules. You must include the car model, its licence plate, its "taxable horsepower", how many months you owned it in 2007, your share in it if jointly owned and the year it was first acquired, by you or someone else.

d) For leisure craft falling under the imputed income criteria, you need to include the name, number and port where it is registered, the country, days of ownership during 2007, length, husband's and wife's share (in case of co-ownership) and date of registration. Below that, in boxes 731-732, you must record the wages paid to the leisure craft's crew.

e) If you own a plane or helicopter, you declare its place of registration, model, constructor's serial number, main airport of call, months of ownership in 2007, horsepower or pounds of engine thrust, registration date and, finally, the imputed expenditure (boxes 715-716).

f) Pool owners must indicate whether it is an indoor or outdoor one, its size and the ownership share of each spouse.

g) You record the total number of items that fall under the imputed income rules in boxes 795-796.

2. In this section you must record the actual expenditure for:

a) Buying or leasing of cars, motorcycles and other vehicles (719-720).

b) Buying or leasing of leisure craft and aircraft (721-722).

c) Buying or leasing of movable property worth over 5,000 euros (723-724).

d) Buying, leasing of, or timesharing in, properties (735-736).

e) Construction costs for all types of buildings, as well as pools (737-738).

f) For gifts and donations to children, parents and other organisations, except the state and local authorities (725-726).

g) For the repayment of the principal of loans and other credit, including credit card payments for the acquisition of non-consumer goods (727-728)

Table 6: Tax breaks

ΠΙΝΑΚΑΣ 6. ΠΡΟΣΘΕΤΑ ΠΛΗΡΟΦΟΡΙΑΚΑ ΣΤΟΙΧΕΙΑ - ΠΟΣΑ ΠΟΥ ΜΕΙΩΝΟΥΝ ΤΗΝ ΕΤΗΣΙΑ ΔΑΠΑΝΗ					
1. Καθαρό εισόδημα που δεν υπήρχε την 1-1-2007			655	656	
2. Ποσό ετήσιας δαπάνης που δεν υπήρχε την 1-1-2007			693	694	
3. Εισοδήματα που αποκτήσατε το 2006, τα οποία απαλλάσσονται από το φόρο, φορολογούνται με ειδικό τρόπο, καθώς και από μερίσματα ημεδαπών Α.Ε. κτλ.			659	660	
4. Καθαρά κέρδη από εταιρίες κτλ., που φορολογήθηκαν με το άρθρο 10 Κ.Φ.Ε. και από Ε.Π.Ε.			431	432	
5. Φόρος που παρακρατήθηκε στα εισοδήματα της περ. 3 και στα καθαρά κέρδη της περ. 4			433	434	
6. Ενοίκιο εγκατάστασης ατομικής επιχείρησης ή ελευθέριου επαγγέλματος					
Ονοματεπώνυμα ή Επωνυμία εκμισθωτή	Κ.Α.	Α.Φ.Μ. εκμισθωτή	Επιφάνεια σε τ.μ.		
	790			793	794
	791			615	616
	810			829	830
	418			469	470
7. Ενοίκιο ακινήτων εκτός από κύρια κατοικία, κατοικία παιδιών που σπουδάζουν και περίπτ. 6					
	417			419	420
8. Χρηματικά ποσά που προέρχονται από διάθεση περιουσιακών στοιχείων, εισαγωγή χρηματικών κεφαλαίων αλλοδαπής, δάνεια, δωρεές κτλ.			781	782	
9. Ανάλωση κεφαλαίου που ήδη φορολογήθηκε ή απαλλασσόταν από το φόρο			787	788	

1. Net income source existing in 2007 but not after January 1, 2008 (you estimate it) (655-656).

2. Expenditure falling into the imputed category and that no longer exists after January 1, 2008 (693-694).

3. Income earned in 2007 that is tax-exempt or taxed at a special rate; also income from domestic companies; dividends (659-660). These are incomes such as wages given to the blind or those with severe motor disabilities, pensions to war invalids, the lifetime pensions to mothers of at least three children etc.

4. Net income from participation in partnership and limited liability companies (431-432).

5. Tax withheld for incomes declared under (3) and the net income in case (4) (433-434).

6. Rent paid for space used for exercising a professional activity or as company headquarters.

7. Rent for premises other than residence.

8. Money from the sale of property (proof required), importation of capital, earnings from games of chance.

9. Expenditure from capital accumulated before 2007.

Table 7: Tax-exempt expenditure

1. Spending on hospitalisation and/or medical care (boxes 061-052).

2. Contributions to social security funds (053-054).

3. Donations of medical equipment to hospitals (057-058).

4. Donations to the public sector, welfare institutions over 100 euros (059-060).

5. Donations to non-profit private organisations over 100 euros (061-062).

6. Interest paid on housing loans for a main residence. For loans contracted after January 1, 2000, you need to declare the size of the property in square metres (063-070).

7. Payment of rents. You need your landlord's ΑΦΜ, which you have in the contract you signed. You must produce receipts of the rent. It is better to keep all of them, although, in reality, tax offices accept the first and last receipts of the year as proof of habitation throughout the year.

8. Rent you pay for your children that study abroad. As in (7) you need proof of payment.

9. Insurance payments (life, accident, health). You need proof of payment provided by the insurance company.

10. Alimony paid by spouse.

11. Spending on natural gas installation.

12. Fees to cramming schools paid for each child.

You need receipts for all the above.

Table 8: Pre-paid taxes

ΠΙΝΑΚΑΣ 8. ΠΡΟΚΑΤΑΒΛΗΘΕΝΤΕΣ - ΠΑΡΑΚΡΑΤΗΘΕΝΤΕΣ ΦΟΡΟΙ			
1. Φόροι 4%, 10%, που προκαταβλήθηκαν (άρθρο 52 Κ.Φ.Ε.)	601	,	602
2. Φόροι 1%, 3%, 4%, 8%, 15% και 20% που παρακρατήθηκαν (άρθρο 55 Κ.Φ.Ε.)	603	,	604
3. Φόροι 20% (άρθρο 58 Κ.Φ.Ε.) και 15% (παρ. 3 άρθρου 7 ν. 2753/1999) που παρακρατήθηκαν	605	,	606
4. Φόρος που καταλογίστηκε για ωφέλεια από πώληση αυτοκινήτου επιχείρησης	607	,	608
5. Φόρος που παρακρατήθηκε στις αμοιβές της περίπτ. 5 του Πίν. 4Α	609	,	610
6. Φόρος που καταβλήθηκε στο εξωτερικό	651	,	652
7. Φόρος που καταβλήθηκε στο εξωτερικό για εισοδήματα της περίπτ. 9 του πίν.4Ζ	611	,	612
8. Φόρος που παρακρατήθηκε στα εισοδήματα από τόκους δανείων κτλ. ημεδαπής (Πίν.4 ΣΤ)	293	,	294
9. Φόρος που αναλογεί στους μισθούς, συντάξεις (περίπτ. 1, 2, 3, 4 και 6 του Πίν. 4Α)	313	,	314
10. Φόρος που παρακρατήθηκε στους μισθούς, συντάξεις (περίπτ. 1, 2, 3, 4 και 6 του Πίν. 4Α)	315	,	316
11. Φόρος που αναλογεί στα εισοδήματα που φορολογούνται με το Ζ Ψήφισμα (βουλευτές κτλ.)	917	,	918
12. Φόρος που παρακρατήθηκε στην Ελλάδα στα εισοδήματα από τόκους, μερίσματα τίτλων κτλ. αλλοδαπής προέλευσης (περίπτ. 8 του Πίν. 4Ζ)	297	,	298

The item of interest to you is probably the sections (9, 10) which refer to taxes withheld at source for wage earners and pensioners. All others are for special cases: architects and engineers (section 1), commercial companies (section 2), self-employed professionals (3), sale of company cars (4), tax paid abroad (6) etc.

Table 9: Dependents

This section is fairly straightforward. Adult children who study cannot be older than 25.

ΠΙΝΑΚΑΣ 9. ΣΤΟΙΧΕΙΑ ΠΡΟΣΩΠΩΝ ΠΟΥ ΣΥΝΟΙΚΟΥΝ ΜΕ ΤΟΥΣ ΦΟΡΟΛΟΓΟΥΜΕΝΟΥΣ ΚΑΙ ΤΟΥΣ ΒΑΡΥΝΟΥΝ								
1 Ανήλικα παιδιά που γεννήθηκαν από 1/1/1988 έως 31/12/2006 ή από 1/1/1981 και σπουδάζουν σε αναγνωρισμένες σχολές, καθώς και όσα παιδιά που είναι άνεργα εγγεγραμμένα στους καταλόγους του ΟΑΕΔ. Παιδιά ανάπηρα, διαζευγμένα ή σε κατάσταση χηρείας, με αναπηρία 67% και πάνω, καθώς και ανίκανοι παιδιά που υπηρετούν τη στρατιωτική τους θητεία, ανεξάρτητα από ηλικία				2 α) Ανιόντες των συζύγων (γονείς, παππούδες κτλ.) β) Ανήλικοι συγγενείς μέχρι τον 3ο βαθμό, ορφανοί από πατέρα και μητέρα γ) Ανύπαντροι ή χήροι ή διαζευγμένοι αδελφοί και αδελφές, με αναπηρία 67% και πάνω				
Όνομα	Έτος γέννησης	Σχολή ή σχολείο φοίτησης		Ονοματεπώνυμο	κ.α.	Α.Φ.Μ.	Με Υπόχρεο	Με Σύζυγο
					831			
					832			
					833			
					834			
					835			

Table 10: Taxpayer's data; filled by the tax office.

Table 11

ΠΙΝΑΚΑΣ 11. Αν προκύψει επιστρεφόμενο ποσό να κατατεθεί στον ακόλουθο λογαριασμό μου			
ΤΡΑΠΕΖΑ	ΚΩΔ.		ΑΡΙΘΜΟΣ ΛΟΓΑΡΙΑΣΜΟΥ ΙΒΑΝ

Τα στοιχεία των φορολογουμένων είναι απόρρητα. Διατηρούνται από το Υπουργείο Οικονομίας και Οικονομικών σε αρχεία, που υπάγεται στην Αρχή Προστασίας Δεδομένων Προσωπικού Χαρακτήρα και λειτουργεί σύμφωνα με το ν.2472/1997 και τις ειδικές ρυθμίσεις των φορολογικών νόμων. Κάθε φορολογούμενος έχει δικαίωμα πρόσβασης στα στοιχεία που τον αφορούν.

Ο ΕΛΕΓΞΑΣ	Ημερομηνία παραλαβής 2007	Ο ΛΟΓΙΣΤΗΣ		2007
	Ο ΠΑΡΑΛΑΒΩΝ	Επων.:	Αρμόδια Δ.Ο.Υ. :	Ο ΔΗΛΩΝ Η ΔΗΛΟΥΣΑ
		Όνομ.:	Αρ. Μητρ. αδ. ασκ. επαγγ/τος:	
		Δ/νση :	Κατηγορία άδειας :	
		Α.Φ.Μ.:		

If you think you are owed a tax return (which is very likely if you are a salaried employee) you write the name of the bank and the account number to which your tax return will be deposited.

Filling in the E9

If you own property, chances are you need to file the E9 form with your E1. Here is how to fill it out

The E9 form records your property holdings. You file it together with the main form, E1, in duplicate if you submit your income declaration in paper form. You may submit it somewhat later if filing online.

Who fills in the E9

If you do not own any property, or there has been no change in your property holdings in 2007, you are not required to file the E9 form.

You must file the E9 form if
● You acquired any property or the use of property (for example, if a parent or child acquired the property and turned it over to you to use over your lifetime)

- There have been any changes made in the property or properties declared in previous years
- There have been changes in the family: for instance, if a man has married a woman who owns property; if a couple where both are property owners has divorced or separated; if the property owner has died; and if children who are property owners or users and had been declared as protected members no longer have such status, either because they have become adults - reached 18 years of age or 25 if they are students. Males serving in the army as conscripts are also considered protected members, irrespective of age

You do not have to submit any documents proving your ownership of the property with the E9 form.

Page 1

In a beehive of six boxes on the top left of page 1 of the form, you are asked whether you declared any property in either 2006 or 2007. If yes, cross out the NAI column with an X.

The set of boxes on the right asks whether the 2008 declaration is: initial, supplementary, recall or provisional. Cross out the relevant box (in almost all cases under initial - APXIKH).

The table containing line 1 is filled with information about the property owner (tax number - AΦM, last name, first name, father's name). The last two columns are filled only if the property owner has died (next to last column) or, if the property owner is a company, it has ceased to exist (last column). For convenience, we will assume we are referring to individual property owners from now on.

In the following table, containing lines 2-10, you are asked to record your spouse or children, only if they own property themselves. You are asked for their AΦM, last name (as recorded in their ID document), name, father's name and relationship to you (whether spouse or child). In their last three columns, you are asked to record any change in relationship, either because you are including them for the first time or because they are delisted (due to death or other reasons).

If the E9 form is not submitted by you but by an authorised representative, his/her data (capacity, ΑΦΜ, last name, first name, father's name, ID number) are entered in the following table.

E9	ΔΗΛΩΣΗ

ΣΤΟΙΧΕΙΩΝ ΑΚΙΝΗΤΩΝ

που υπάρχουν την 1η Ιανουαρίου 2007

ΥΠΟΒΑΛΛΕΤΑΙ ΣΕ ΔΥΟ (2) ΑΝΤΙΤΥΠΑ

Προς τη Δ. Ο. Υ. ....

ΑΡΙΘΜΟΣ ΔΗΛΩΣΗΣ*
ΑΡΙΘΜΟΣ ΦΑΚΕΛΟΥ*

Δηλώθηκαν ακίνητα στο Ε9 έτους

2005	ΝΑΙ	ΟΧΙ
2006	ΝΑΙ	ΟΧΙ

ΕΙΔΟΣ ΔΗΛΩΣΗΣ ΕΤΟΥΣ 2007

ΑΡΧΙΚΗ	ΣΥΜΠΛΗΡΩΜΑΤΙΚΗ ΤΡΟΠΟΠΟΙΗΤΙΚΗ	ΑΝΑΚΛΗΤΙΚΗ	ΜΕ ΕΠΙΦΥΛΑΞΗ

ΣΤΟΙΧΕΙΑ ΤΟΥ ΥΠΟΧΡΕΟΥ (Με κεφαλαία)

ΚΩΔΙΚΟΣ ΑΡΙΘΜΟΣ ΙΔΙΟΚΤΗΤΗ	ΑΦΜ	ΕΠΩΝΥΜΟ ή ΕΠΩΝΥΜΙΑ	ΟΝΟΜΑ	ΠΑΤΡΩΝΥΜΟ	ΔΙΑΓΡΑΦΗ ΛΟΓΩ	
					ΘΑΝΑΤΟΥ Φ.Π.	ΔΙΑΚΟΠΗΣ ΕΡΓΑΣΙΩΝ (κ.λ.π.) Ν.Π.
1.						

ΣΤΟΙΧΕΙΑ ΣΥΖΥΓΟΥ ΚΑΙ ΠΡΟΣΤΑΤΕΥΟΜΕΝΩΝ ΤΕΚΝΩΝ ΠΟΥ ΕΧΟΥΝ ΟΠΟΙΟΔΗΠΟΤΕ ΕΜΠΡΑΓΜΑΤΟ ΔΙΚΑΙΩΜΑ ΣΕ ΑΚΙΝΗΤΟ

ΚΩΔΙΚΟΣ ΑΡΙΘΜΟΣ ΙΔΙΟΚΤΗΤΗ	ΑΦΜ	ΕΠΩΝΥΜΟ (Όπως στην ταυτότητα)	ΟΝΟΜΑ	ΠΑΤΡΩΝΥΜΟ	ΣΧΕΣΗ ΜΕ ΤΟΝ ΥΠΟΧΡΕΟ		ΜΕΤΑΒΟΛΗ ΣΧΕΣΗΣ		
					ΣΥΖ	ΤΕΚ.	ΕΙΣΑΓΩΓΗ	ΔΙΑΓΡΑΦΗ	
								ΛΟΓΩ ΘΑΝΑΤΟΥ	ΑΛΛΗ ΑΙΤΙΑ
2.									
3.									
4.									
5.									
6.									
7.									
8.									
9.									
10.									

ΣΤΟΙΧΕΙΑ ΝΟΜΙΜΟΥ ΕΚΠΡΟΣΩΠΟΥ ή ΑΝΤΙΚΛΗΤΟΥ

ΙΔΙΟΤΗΤΑ	ΑΦΜ	ΕΠΩΝΥΜΟ	ΟΝΟΜΑ	ΠΑΤΡΩΝΥΜΟ	ΑΡΙΘΜ. ΤΑΥΤΟΤΗΤΑΣ

ΣΗΜΕΙΩΣΕΙΣ ΦΟΡΟΛΟΓΟΥΜΕΝΟΥ :

* Όσα τετραγωνίδια έχουν αστερίσκο θα συμπληρωθούν από την υπηρεσία

The first page also includes space for any notes you need to write to explain things that cannot be entered in the other tables.

Pages 2 and 3

Pages 2 and 3 of the form contain two tables in which you describe in detail your properties, including any that you sold last year. The first table is for land and buildings within areas zoned as urban. The second table is for land plots located outside built areas, labelled, for convenience, "farm parcels" (although you are asked in the table to precisely label the kind of land you own).

If your property contains other built spaces besides a house (eg for storage or a closed parking space) these are declared on a separate line as distinct properties. The same holds true for the "air rights" (that is, the right to add floors to your building).

Table 1 contains the following columns:

Column (1) Property identification number - to be filled in by the tax office, not you.

Column (2) Serial number. Enter properties belonging to the persons identified on Page 1, by year and order of acquisition. For example, if you only own one property, which you acquired in 2007, write 20071. If you acquired a second property, identify it as 20072 etc. If you already own a property that you bought in 2004, for example, list it first as 20041. Further down, list in chronological order all properties you subsequently acquired.

An exception to the above numbering rule concerns property acquired by a spouse in 2007, whom you subsequently married (or were divorced or separated from) or by a protected family member who ceased to be one last year. In this case, the code for the properties acquired is 20081, 20082 (instead of 20071, 20072).

Columns (3)-(6): Address
(3) Prefecture.
(4) Municipality.
(5) Road and number.

(6) Frontage - mark this with an X.

Column (7) Other roads bordering the block. Write the roads bordering your city block and, if your property has a frontage on any of those, add an X to the column next to the road.

Column (8) Block number. This information should be on your property deed. Otherwise, ask your municipality, or local tax authority.

Column (9) Type of property. Enter the proper code. These codes (which you can also find on the back page of the form are [1] for apartments, [2] for a single house, [3] for commercial use (for multi-use properties see codes 7-11), [4] for non-built land plots, [5] storage spaces (if separate buildings), [6] parking space (on an unbuilt plot), [7] parking stations, [8] factories, [9] tourist installations, hospitals and foundations, [10] schools, [11] sports facilities, [12] any other buildings (eg churches, museums, cinemas etc).

Column (10) Special circumstances. Again, this is a multi-code column with separate codes for [1] buildings under expropriation, as well as those for which a demolition permit has been issued, [2] a plot under expropriation, [3] a listed building, [4] tied-up property or suspended construction due to archaeological findings, [5] a plot that cannot be built but can be exchanged, [6] a plot that can neither be built nor exchanged [99] unfinished construction.

Column (11) Floor. Write Y for basement, 0 for ground floor, 1 for first floor etc. In case of a multi-floor apartment (maisonette), write the higher floor.

Columns (12)-(17) concern the building itself.

(12) Floor space of main part of the house (in square metres).

(13) Size of auxiliary areas... Do not include areas that can be listed separately.

(14) Year of construction.

(15) Type of ownership. Use codes for [1] full ownership, [2]

ΠΙΝΑΚΑΣ 1: ΣΤΟΙΧΕΙΑ ΟΙΚΟΠΕΔΩΝ (ΕΝΤΟΣ ΣΧΕΔΙ... ΚΑΙ ΚΤΙΣΜΑΤΩΝ (ΕΝΤΟΣ & ΕΚΤΟΣ ΣΧΕ...)

ΑΡΙΘΜΟΣ ΤΑΥΤΟΤΗΤΑΣ ΑΚΙΝΗΤΟΥ (*) (1)	Α/Α (2)	ΝΟΜΟΣ (3)	ΔΗΜΟΣ / ΔΙΑΜΕΡΙΣΜΑ ή ΚΟΙΝΟΤΗΤΑ (4)	ΟΔΟΣ - ΑΡΙΘΜΟΣ (5)	Π. (6)	ΟΔΟΣ (7)	Π. (6)	ΟΔΟΣ (7)	Π. (6)	ΟΔΟΣ (7)	Π. (6)	ΑΡΙΘΜΟΣ ΟΙΚΟΔΟΜΙΚΟΥ ΤΕΤΡΑΓΩΝΟΥ (8)	ΚΑΤΗΓΟΡΙΑ ΑΚΙΝΗΤΟΥ (9)	ΕΙΔΙΚΩΝ ΣΥΝΘΗΚΩΝ (10)	ΟΡΟΦΟΣ (11)

152

(12) ΚΥΡΙΟΙ ΧΩΡΟΙ	(13) ΒΟΗΘΗΤΙΚΟΙ ΧΩΡΟΙ	(14) ΕΤΟΣ ΚΑΤΑΣΚΕΥΗΣ	(15) ΕΙΔΟΣ ΕΜΠ/ΓΟΥ ΔΙΚΑΙΩΜΑΤΟΣ	(16) ΠΟΣΟΣΤΟ ΣΥΝΙΔΙΟΚΤΗΣΙΑΣ %	(17) ΕΤΟΣ ΓΕΝ. ΕΠΙΚΑΡΠΩΤΗ	(18) ΕΠΙΦΑΝΕΙΑ	(19) ΕΙΔΟΣ ΕΜΠ/ΓΟΥ ΔΙΚΑΙΩΜΑΤΟΣ	(20) ΠΟΣΟΣΤΟ ΣΥΝΙΔΙΟΚΤΗΣΙΑΣ %	(21) ΕΤΟΣ ΓΕΝ. ΕΠΙΚΑΡΠΩΤΗ	(22) ΣΥΝΟΛΙΚΗ ΕΠΙΦΑΝ. ΚΤΙΣΜΑΤΩΝ ΣΤΟ ΟΙΚΟΠΕΔΟ	(23) ΚΔΑ. ΑΡΙΘΜΟΣ ΙΔΙΟΚΤΗΤΗ	(24) ΚΩΔΙΚΟΣ ΜΕΤΑΒΟΛΗΣ

(ΚΤΙΣΜΑ: columns 12–17; ΟΙΚΟΠΕΔΟ: columns 18–21)

ownership without use, [3] use of property without ownership (in legalese called usufruct, ie the right to use and derive profit or benefit from property that belongs to another person) or residence.

(16) Percentage of ownership or co-ownership. Up to five decimals.

(17) Year of usufructuary's birth (if applicable).

Columns (18) - (21) Apply to land plots.

(18) Area.
(19) As in (15).
(20) As in (16).
(21) As in (17).

ΠΙΝΑΚΑΣ 2: ΣΤ...

ΑΡΙΘΜΟΣ ΤΑΥΤΟΤΗΤΑΣ ΑΚΙΝΗΤΟΥ (*) (1)	Α/Α (2)	ΔΙΕΥΘΥΝΣΕΙΣ ΑΚΙΝΗΤΩΝ			Η ΕΛΑΦΙΚΗ ΕΚΤΑΣΗ ΣΕ ΟΔΟ ΕΧΕΙ ΠΡΟΣΟΨΗ (6)	ΑΠΟΣΤΑΣΗ ΑΠΟ ΘΑΛΑΣΣΑ (μέχρι 800 μ.) (7)	Η ΕΛΑΦΙΚΗ ΕΚΤΑΣΗ ΕΙΝΑΙ ΑΙΓΙΑΛΟΠΑΡΑΚΤΙΑ (8)	Η ΕΛΑΦΙΚΗ ΕΚΤΑΣΗ ΕΙΝΑΙ ΑΡΔΕΥΟΜΕΝΗ (9)
		ΝΟΜΟΣ (3)	ΔΗΜΟΣ / ΔΙΑΜΕΡΙΣΜΑ ή ΚΟΙΝΟΤΗΤΑ (4)	ΟΔΟΣ - ΑΡΙΘΜΟΣ ή ΘΕΣΗ (5)				

Ημερομηνία παραλαβής 2007

Ο ΠΑΡΑΛΑΒΩΝ

(*) Παρατήρηση : Τα τετράγωνα αυτά θα συμπληρωθούν από την υπηρεσία

ΕΠΙΦΑΝΕΙΑ ΣΕ ΤΕΤΡΑΓΩΝΙΚΑ ΜΕΤΡΑ

ΜΟΝΟΕΤΗΣ ΚΑΛΛΙΕΡΓΕΙΑ	ΠΟΛΥΕΤΗΣ ΚΑΛΛΙΕΡΓΕΙΑ		ΒΟΣΚΟΤΟΠΟΣ	ΔΑΣΙΚΗ ΕΚΤΑΣΗ	ΜΕΤΑΛΛΕΥΤΙΚΗ ή ΛΑΤΟΜΙΚΗ	ΥΠΑΙΘΡΙΑ ΕΚΘΕΣΗ ή ΧΩΡΟΣ ΣΤΑΘΜΕΥ.ΣΗΣ	ΣΥΝΟΛΙΚΗ ΕΠΙΦΑΝΕΙΑ ΚΤΙΣΜΑΤΩΝ ΠΟΥ ΒΡΙΣΚΟΝΤΑΙ ΣΤΟ ΑΓΡΟΧΙΟ	ΕΙΔΟΣ ΕΜΠ/ΤΟΥ ΔΙΚΑΙΩ-ΜΑΤΟΣ	ΠΟΣΟΣΤΟ ΣΥΝΙΔΙΟ-ΚΤΗΣΙΑΣ %	ΕΤΟΣ ΓΕΝ. ΕΠΙΚΑΡ-ΠΩΤΗ	ΚΩΔ. ΑΡΙΘΜΟΣ ΙΔΙΟ-ΚΤΗΤΗ	ΚΩΔ. ΜΕΤΑ-ΒΟΛΗΣ
	ΕΛΙΕΣ	ΛΟΙΠΕΣ ΔΕΝΔΡΟΚΑΛ-ΛΙΕΡΓΕΙΕΣ										
(10)	(11)	(12)	(13)	(14)	(15)	(16)	(17)	(18)	(19)	(20)	(21)	(22)

Ημερομηνία 2007

Ο ΔΗΛΩΝ   Η ΣΥΖΥΓΟΣ

ή ΑΝΤΙΠΡΟΣΩΠΟΣ   ή ΚΗΔΕΜΟΝΑΣ

Column (22) Total area of buildings in the plot.

Column (23) Owner's code number (the number given on page 1).

Column (24) Change code. [1] for a new property, [2] for changes in an already declared property and [3] for delisting a property.

Table 2 contains the following columns.

Column (1) Property identification number. Same as (1) in Table 1.

Column (2) Serial number. Same as (2) in Table 1.

Columns (3)-(5) concern the address of the property and are similar to (3)-(5) in Table 1. Since these are land plots outside built areas and may lack a road address number, you can put in a location under (5).

Column (6) Asks whether the property faces a road. If so, put [1] if it faces a national or regional road, [2] if it faces a municipal road or a commonly used space (with the exception of a sea or beach), [3] if it faces a farm path or private path/road (not a beach) and [4] if it is completely surrounded by other property without a path leading to it (ie if it is "blind" in real-estate parlance).

Column (7) Asks whether the plot is within 800 metres of the sea. If so, put in the distance.

Column (8) Asks whether the plot is under expropriation. If yes, mark the blank with an X.

Column (9) Asks whether the plot is irrigated. If so, put in an X.

Columns (10)-(16) concern area and land use. You write the area, in square metres, where it applies to you.

(10) Annual crops.

(11)-(12) Multi-year crops [trees]: (11) is for olives and (12) for all other types of trees.

(13) Grazing land.

(14) Forest.

(15) Mining (including strip mining).

(16) Other open areas (including for parking).

Column (17) Total area of buildings in the plot.

Column (18) Same as (19) in Table 1.

Column (19) Same as (20) in Table 1.

Column (20) Same as (21) in Table 1.

Column (21) Same as (23) in Table 1.

Column (22) Same as (24) in Table 1.

Those whose property is valued at over 243,600 euros (single) or 487,200 euros (married) are also obliged to submit a special Large Ownership Tax form, irrespective of changes in the status of their property.

If you have any questions about the E9 form, you can call the ministry of finance helpline at 210-337-5360 or 210-325-3748.

Inheritance

If you inherit a property or other assets, you must declare it within six months of the legator's death or the publication of the legator's will (assuming there are no challenges in court). If you were residing abroad at the time of the legator's death, you can declare the inheritance within a year. The tax authorities can grant you an additional three months, in special circumstances. Failure to declare an inheritance on time results in a fine similar to the one imposed for non-timely declaration of income (a 2.5 percent surcharge per month of delay).

When declaring an inheritance you must submit:

- A notarised death act.
- A will.
- A certificate by a Court of First Instance secretary stating that no other will was written after the one you submitted.
- If there have been delays due to legal challenges, you also need to submit documents proving the legal procedure.
- If the legator has left debts, you also need documentation to prove these debts.

You submit these documents to the legator's local tax office or the foreign residents' tax office, if the legator lived abroad. If the legator was a resident of a foreign country but died in Greece, submit the documents to the tax office closest to the place of death.

A gift from a living parent to a child must also be declared. The total value of parental gifts to children may not exceed 100,000 euros by either parent, if they are alive, or 130,000 euros, if one of the parents is deceased.

If your deceased parent bequeaths you a residence, you are exempt from inheritance tax if you do not already own either a residence that covers your and your family's needs or a property on which you can build a residence that covers those needs. You are also exempt if you do own such a property/residence in a municipality with fewer than 3,000 residents.

The inheritance tax is paid in 24 instalments, every two months over four years. If the inheritor is a minor, it can be paid in 48 instalments. But, if there has been a dispute that required an administrative court decision to determine the inheritance, the tax is paid in six instalments, at most.

The E3

The E3 form is submitted by professionals and businesses. For the purposes of this article, we assume you are an individual deriving part of your income from a professional activity.

The E3 should be submitted together with the E1 in paper form (two copies) or electronically, according to the E1 form deadlines.

Not all of the tables apply to you. The ones that do are the first seven (A-Z).

At the very top of the form (boxes 002-003), enter the financial year the declaration applies to. You should write 1/1/2007 (box 002) and 31/12/2007 (box 003).

You also fill boxes 005 (tax office to which you submit the form) and, if different in the previous year, 007. If you happen to file an additional E3 form (a very rare occurrence), put a cross (ΤΡΟΠ/ΚΗ) in box 008 if the additional form revises the original one or on (ΑΝΑΚΛΗΤΙΚΗ) if it recalls the original one, that is, you file again from scratch.

As a professional you are obliged to keep accounting books (Category B). Thus, in box 019 cross out (B).

Box 726 asks you whether you are exempt from keeping accounting books for some reason. Most likely you are not. If in doubt, ask the tax office or a professional.

In box 730, enter a 1, unless (an extremely rare case) you have chosen to report on more than one financial year.

Enter your personal data in Table A. If you are a married couple submitting a joint declaration and it is the wife that pursues a professional activity, fill in the husband's data (ΑΦΜ and name) in box 041.

In box 761, enter the code indicating the type of professional activity you pursued in 2007. These codes are included in the booklet you received together with the forms in the mail. In the unlikely event that you did not receive the booklet and forms, both are available at the local tax office. If you pursued several activities, enter the code for the activity that generated the most income.

In Table B enter the types of receipts you issued for payment for your services. In the first column, specify whether you issue receipts or invoices (professionals usually issue only receipts) and, in the second and third, enter the serial number of the first and last receipt you issued during the year.

Table Γ most likely does not apply to you, unless you have branches or storage rooms, or employ permanent or seasonal personnel. In the event that you trade goods and services online, you must fill in boxes 076 (for goods) and 077 (for services) crossing out the NAI column.

Table Δ applies only to businesses, unless you have decided to entrust the filling of the form to a representative or an accountant.

Table E is for those of you who either received subsidies for your activity (boxes 681 and 904) or who paid rent for the location of your professional activities. If you worked from home, do not fill in the boxes.

Table ΣT concerns, specifically, small businesses and professionals.

Section (a) asks you to record any purchases of goods you made. As a professional, you are really only concerned about perishable goods (boxes 239 and 240, the latter in case you imported them), parts for fixed goods (boxes 243 and 244) and any fixed assets you use for your professional activity (811 and 812).

Sections (β) and (γ) are for companies. In section (δ), you must declare any expenses in the form of salaries to personnel (box 524), fees to third parties (527) and other expenses (536). Add up these expenses in box 546. (We did not include all the boxes because it is very unlikely you will have expenses of this nature.)

Sections (ε) and (στ) also concern companies.

In section (ζ) enter the income you earned from selling your professional services to individuals (box 274), the public sector (277) or other professionals and companies (280). Box 275 is for engineers' draft work (eg a civil engineer's design of a residence, an electrical engineer's design of a building's electricity systems etc). If your income source is not from any of the above sources, declare it in box 278.

Section (η) asks you to enter the revenue declared in (ζ), as well as any expenses declared in (a) and (δ). In box 551 enter the revenue declared in box 283. All expenses declared in box

559 and the net result in boxes 563 and 571 unless you also have expenses that are not deducted from your income (567 - do not enter anything here).

Table Z is strictly for special cases, such as people whose activity is subsidised by the investments incentives law (also called the development law) or research scientists.

❏ UTILITIES

HELLENIC TELECOMMUNICATIONS ORGANISATION (OTE)

Telephone (phone repair hotline)	121
Within Greece Call Information	129
International Call Information (English, French & German)	139
Information on OTE Subscribers	11888
OTE Customer Service	134
INFOTE (YELLOW PAGES)	11811
TELEX	187
TELEGRAM SERVICE (DOMESTIC)	155
TELEGRAM SERVICE (INTERNATIONAL)	165

PUBLIC POWER CORPORATION (DEI) www.dei.gr

General Information	10500
Athens	10503
Mesogion	10506
Northern Suburbs	10508
Peristeri	10505
Piraeus	10504
Southern Suburbs	10509

DEI offices around Greece

Attica: 5-7 Aristidou St, Athens 105 59, tel 210 328 7100, fax 210 328 7391, astil@tee.gr

Macedonia/Thrace: 9A Ethnikis Aminis St, Thessaloniki 546 21, tel 2310 360000, fax 2310 224770, papanikolaou@deinet.gr

Peloponnese/Epirus: 15 Akti Dimeon St, Patra 262 22, tel 2610 311111, fax 2610-329835, dehdpp@otenet.gr

Central Greece: 36 Othonos St, Lamia 351 00, tel 22310 25531-8, fax 22310 25460, deidpk@yahoo.gr

Islands: 112 Syngrou Ave, Athens 117 41, tel 210 923 8711-9, 210 923 8901-3, fax 210 922 4336, msideris@dpn. gr

WATER SUPPLY & SEWERAGE (EYDAP) www.eydap.gr

Sewerage of Attica - Switchboard	210 749 5555
Customer Service	1022

GAS DELIVERY (EPA) www.aerioattikis.gr

Gas information-failures	1133

POSTAL SERVICES www.elta.gr

General information	800 11 82000

❏ AIRPORTS

Aktion/Preveza,	tel 26820 22089
Alexandroupolis,	tel 25510 89300
Athens International Airport	
Elefthereios Venizelos,	tel 210 353 0000
Astypalea,	tel 22430 61410
Corfu,	tel 26610 89600
Hania,	tel 28210 63224
Hios,	tel 22710 44260
Ikaria,	tel 22750 32216
Ioannina,	tel 26510 27058
Iraklio,	tel 2810 228401
Kalamata,	tel 27210 63805
Karpathos,	tel 22450 23101-2
Kassos,	tel 22450 41587
Kastelorizo,	tel 22460 49250
Kastoria,	tel 24670 42515

Kavala,	tel 2510 53271-2
Kefalonia,	tel 26710 29900
Kos,	tel 22420 56000
Kozani,	tel 24610 36098
Kythira,	tel 27360 38395-8
Leros,	tel 22470 22275
Limnos,	tel 22540 29400
Milos,	tel 22870 22090
Mykonos,	tel 22890 22489
Mytilini,	tel 22510 38700
Naxos	tel 22850 23969
Paros,	tel 22840 91256
Rhodes,	tel 22410 83200
Samos,	tel 22730 87800
Santorini,	tel 22860 31525
Sitia,	tel 28430 24424
Skiathos,	tel 24270 22376
Skyros,	tel 22220 91607
Syros,	tel 22810 82255
Thessaloniki,	tel 2310 473 212/473 312
Zakynthos,	tel 26950 29500

❑ PUBLIC SERVICES

Citizens' Information Centre (multilingual,
seven days a week, 24 hours a day)   1564
State Certificate Issue Office
(on weekdays 8am-8pm)   1502
Attica Customs, Ag Nikolaou Sq, Piraeus   210 428 4475
Hellenic Tourist Organisation (EOT) www.eot.gr
                    210 870 7000, fax 210 644-2926

Tourist Information Service ELPA	10400
Tourist Police	171
Time	141
Wake-up Call	1402

WEATHER & POLLUTION
Attica/Greece (in Greek)	1448

LOTTERY www.opap.gr
Lotto, Proto, Joker (in Greek)	1444
National and Popular Lottery (in Greek)	1445

STOCK MARKET www.ase.gr
Stock Market Shares (recording in Greek)	1424

CENTRAL ALIENS' BUREAU   210 340 5969

❏ CITIZENS' RIGHTS

Ombudsman, 5 Hatziyiannis Mexis St, Athens 11528
(near the Hilton Hotel), tel 210 728 9640,
fax 210 729 2129 website www.synigoros.gr
Consumers' Institute (INKA), 7 Akadimias St,
Athens 106 71, tel 11721, 210 363 2443,
fax 210 363 3976, email inka@inka.gr,
website www.inka.gr
Greek Consumers' Organisation - Quality of Life (EKPIZO),
43-45 Valtetsiou St, Athens 106 81, tel 210 330 4444,
fax 210 330 0591, email ekpizo@ath.forthnet.gr;
info@ekpizo.gr; www.ekpizo.gr
Consumer Protection Centre (KEPKA) 54 Tsimiski St,
Thessaloniki 54 623, tel 2310 233333,
2310 269449, 801 11 17200, fax 2310 242211,
email consumers@kepka.org, www.kepka.gr

Doctors of the World, 12 Sapfous St, Athens 105 53, tel 210 321 3150, fax 210 321 3850, email info@mdmgreece.gr
In Thessaloniki, 65 Ionos Dragoumi St, Thessaloniki 546 30, tel/fax 2310 566641, email mdmthe@otenet.gr; www.mdmgreece.gr
Doctors Without Borders, 15 Xenias St, Athens 115 27, tel 210 5200 500, fax 210 520 0503
Greek Council for Refugees, 25 Solomou St, Athens 106 81, tel 210 332 0000, fax 210 380 3774, email gcr1@gcr.gr
Network for the Support of Immigrants and Refugees, 48b, 3rd September St, Athens, tel 210 381 3928, fax 210 384 0350

UNITED NATIONS
UNEP/MAP (United Nations Environment Programme/ Mediterranean Action Plan) 48 Vas Konstantinou St, Athens 116 35, tel 210 727 3100, fax 210 725 3196/7, email unepmedu@unepmap.gr; www.unepmap.gr
UNESCO (United Nations Educational, Scientific and Cultural Organisation), 3 Akadimias St, Athens 106 71, tel 210 368 2395-6, fax 210 368 2384
UNHCR (United Nations High Commissioner for Refugees), 23 Taygetou St, P Psyhiko 154 52, tel 210 672 6462, fax 210 675 6800, www.unhcr.gr
UNICEF (United Nations Children's Fund), 8 A Dimitriou & 37 J Kennedy sts, Kaisariani 161 21, tel 210 725 5555, fax 210 725 2555, email unicefgr@hol.gr www.unicef.gr
UNIDO/ITPO (United Nations Industrial Development Organisation/Investment & Technical Investment Promotion Service), 7 Stadiou St, Athens 105 62, tel 210 324 8319, 210 324 8367, fax 210 324 8778,

email unido-athens@ath. forthnet.gr; itpo.athens@unido.org;
www.unido.org
**WHO/MZCC (World Health Organisation/Mediterranean
Zoonoses Control Centre)**, 24 Stournari St, Athens 106 82,
tel 210 381 5179, 210 381 4703, fax 210 381 4340,
email mzcc@ath.forthnet.gr; www.unido.org

❏ GOVERNMENT

President of the Hellenic Republic
Presidential Palace, 2 Vas Georgeio II, tel 210 728 3111,
fax 210 724 8938
Prime Minister
email primeminister@primeminister. gr
Maximos House, 19 Irodou Attikou St, Athens 106 74,
tel 210 338 5491, fax 210 323 8129,
www.primeminister.gr
Ministry for the Aegean & Island Policy
email Info@Ypai. gr Athens Office: 9 Filellinon St, Athens
105 57, tel 210 331 1714/16
Mytilini Office: 2 Mikras Asias St,
Mytilini 811 00, tel 22510 38200, www.ypai.gr
Ministry of Culture
email generalenquiries@noc.culture.gr tel 210 820 1100,
20-22 Bouboulinas St, 10682 Athens www.culture.gr
Ministry of Development
email Grafyp@ypan. gr, tel 210 696 9218, 210 697 4801,
210 697 4803, 119 Mesogion Ave, Athens 10192,
www.ypan.gr
Ministry of Economy & Finance
email ypetho@mnec. gr, tel 210 333 2000,
5-7 Nikis St, Syntagma Square, Athens 105 63
www.ypetho.gr

Ministry of Employment & Social Protection
www.labor-ministry.gr tel 210 529 5000,
40 Pireos St, Athens 185 40,
Ministry for the Environment,
Physical Planning & Public Works
email service@dorg.minenv.gr, tel 210 641 5700,
17 Amaliados, Athens 115 23, www.minenv.gr
Ministry of Foreign Affairs
email cio@mfa.gr, tel 210 368 2700, fax 210 368 1811,
210 368 1821, 3 Akadimias St, Stoa Davaki,
Athens 106 71, www.mfa.gr
Ministry of Health and Social Solidarity
email webmaster@mohaw.gr, tel 210 523 2820/9,
fax 210 523 5749, 19 Aristotelous St, Athens 104 33
www.mohaw.gr
Ministry of Interior, Public Administration and Decentralisation
email pressoffice2@ypes.gr; info@ypes.gr,
tel 210 322 3521/9, 210 323 5612/9,
fax 210 323 3218, 37 Stadiou & 2 Dragatsaniou sts,
Athens 101 83, www.ypes.gr
Ministry of Justice
email minjust@otenet.gr, tel 210 771 1019,
96 Mesogion Ave, Athens 115 27, www.ministryofjustice.gr
Ministry of Macedonia-Thrace
email info@marthra.gr, tel 2310 379000, Dikitiriou Square,
Thessaloniki 541 23, www.marthra.gr
Ministry of Merchant Marine
email egov@mail.yen.gr, tel 210 419 1700, 150 Grigoriou
Lambraki St, Piraeus 185 18 www.yen.gr
Ministry of National Defence
email journalists@mod.gr, tel 210 659 8605,
210 687 6789, 151 Mesogion Ave, Holargos 155 00,
www.mod.gr

Ministry of National Education & Religious Affairs
www.ypepth.gr tel 210 372 3000,
15 Mitropoleos St, Athens 101 85,
Ministry of Public Order
www.ydt.gr tel 210 697 7000,
4 P Kanellopoulou St, Athens 101 77,
Ministry of Rural Development & Food
email info@minagric. gr, tel 210 212 4000,
2 Aharnon St, Athens 104 38, www.minagric.gr
Ministry of Tourism
email info@mintour.gr, tel 210 696 9813-5, 210 870
7605-12, 119 Mesogion Ave, Athens 101 92,
www.mintour.gr
Ministry of Transport & Communications
email yme@yme.gov.gr, tel 210 650 8000
2 Anastaseos St, Papagou 155 61
General Secretariat of Communications
brief@minpress. gr, tel 210 909 8000, fax 210 909 8433,
11 Ragoudi & Alexandrou Pandou sts, Kallithea 101 63,
www.minpress.gr

❏ EMBASSIES

ALBANIA
7 Vekiareli St, Filothei 152 37, tel 210 687 6200,
fax 210 687 6223, email albem@ath.forthnet.gr

ALGERIA
14a, V Konstantinou St, Athens 116 35
tel 210 756 4191-3, fax 210 701 8681-2
email ambdzath@otenet.gr

ANGOLA
24 El Venizelou St, Filothei 152 37, tel 210 681 1994,

fax 210 689 8683, email info@angolanembassy.gr
website angolanembassy.gr

ARGENTINA

59 Vas Sofias Ave, Athens 115 21, tel 210 724 4158,
210 722 4753, 210 722 4710, 210 725 0946,
fax 210 722 7568, email politica@embar.gr;
secretaria@embar.gr   website www.argentinos.gr

AUSTRALIA

Thon Building, cnr Kifissias & Alexandras aves,
Ambelokipi (6th floor), Athens 115 23, tel 210 870 4000,
fax 210 870 4111 (political), 210 870-4055 (consular)
email ae.athens@dfat.gov.au website www.ausemb.gr

AUSTRIA

4 Vas Sofias St, Athens 106 74, tel 210 725 7270,
fax 210 725 7292, email athen-ob@bmaa.gv.at

AZERBAIJAN

10 Skoufa St, Athens 106 73, tel 210 363 2721,
fax 210 363-9087, email az–emb–gr@yahoo.com
website www.azembassy.gr

APOSTOLIC NUNCIATURE

2 Mavili St, PO Box 65075, Paleo Psyhiko154 52,
tel 210 674 3598, 210 672 2728

BANGLADESH CONSULATE

81 Akti Miaouli St, Piraeus 185 38, tel 210 428 3315/7,
fax 210 428 3318, email banglaco@otenet.gr

BELGIUM

3 Sekeri St, Athens 106 71, tel 210 361 7886/7, 210
360 0314-5, 210 338 8540, fax 210 360 4289,
email athens@diplobel.org website www.diplomatie.be/athens

BOSNIA-HERZEGOVINA

25 Filellinon St, Athens 105 57, tel 210 641 0788,

210 641 1375, fax 210 641 1978
email ambasbih@otenet.gr

BRAZIL
14 Platia Philikis Eterias St, Athens 106 73
tel 210 721 3039, 210 723 4450, fax 210 724 4731
email embragre@iembratenas.gr

BULGARIA
33a Stratigou Kallari St, P Psyhiko 154 52,
tel 210 674 8106-7, fax 210 674 8130

CANADA
4, I Gennadiou St, Athens 115 21, tel 210 727 3400,
fax 210 727 3480, email athns@international.gc.ca
website www.athens.gc.ca

CHAD CONSULATE
114 Alimou St, Argyroupoli 164 52, tel 210 992 2774,
fax 210 991 3423, email profthomas2001@yahoo.gr

CHILE
19 Rigillis, Athens 106 74, tel 210 725 2574,
210 729 2647, fax 210 725 2536
email embachilegr1@ath.forthnet.gr

CHINA
10-12 Dimokratias St, P Psyhiko 154 52
tel 210 678 3840, fax 210 672 3819 (chancery),
email chinaemb–gr@mfa.gov.cn website gr.chineseembassy.org
Consular section: 2a Krinon St, P Psyhiko 154 52,
210 672 3282, fax 210 671 8839

CROATIA
4 Tzavela St, N Psyhiko 154 51, tel 210 677 7033,
210 677 7049, 210 677 7037, 210 677 7059,
fax 210 671 1208, email croemb.athens@mvpei.hr

CUBA

5 Sofokleous St, Filothei 152 37, tel 210 685 5550,
fax 210 684 2807, email embacuba@hol.gr
website emba.cubaminrex.cu/greci

CYPRUS

16 Irodotou St, Athens 106 75, tel 210 723 2727,
fax 210 725 8886

CZECH REPUBLIC

6 G Seferi St, P Psyhiko 154 52, tel 210 671 9701,
210 671 3755, fax 210 671 0675,
email athens@embassy.mzv.cz website mzv.cz/athens

DENMARK

10 Mourouzi St, Athens 106 74, tel 210 725 6440,
fax 210 725 6473, email athamb@um.dk
website www.ambathen.um.dk

ECUADOR CONSULATE

6 Sotiros St, Piraeus 185 35, tel 210 422 3800,
fax 210 422 3559

EGYPT

3 Vas Sofias Ave, Athens 106 71, tel 210 361 8612,
210 361 8613, fax 210 360 3538,
email embassyegypt@yahoo.com

ESTONIA

2-4 Mesogion Ave (Athens Tower), Athens 115 27,
tel 210 747 5660, fax 210 747 5661,
email embassy.athens@mfa.ee; www.estemb.gr

ETHIOPIA CONSULATE

253 Syngrou Ave, Athens 171 22, tel 210 940 3483,
210 943 0922, fax 210 942 6050
email ethembath@ath.forthnet.gr

FINLAND

5 Hatzigianni Mexi, Athens 115 28, tel 210 725 5860,
fax 210 725 5864, email sanomat.ate@formin.fi
website www.finland.gr

FRANCE

7 Vas Sofias Ave, Athens 106 71, tel 210 339 1000,
fax 210 339 1009, email ambafran@first.gr
website www.ambafrance-gr.org

GABON CONSULATE

22 K Palaiologou St, Athens 104 38, tel 210 523 6795,
fax 210 522 9138

GEORGIA

24 Ag Dimitriou St, P Psyhiko 154 52, tel 210 674 6332
Honorary Consul of Georgia: 38 Evritanias,
Ambelokipi 115 28, tel 210 748 9180, 210 771 1317,
fax 210 748 9181

GERMANY

3 Karaoli-Dimitriou St, Athens 106 75, tel 210 728 5111,
fax 210 728 5335, email german-embassy@otenet.gr
website www.athen.diplo.de
Honorary Consuls of Germany:
Thessaloniki, tel 2310 251120/251130,
fax 2310 240393, email gkthessaloniki@internet.gr
Iraklio, tel 2810 226288, fax 2810 222141,
email honkons@her.forthnet.gr
Hania, tel 28210 68876, fax 28210 68876
email michael0@otenet.gr
Corfu, tel 26610 36816, fax 26610 36816,
email gisdakis@infoware.gr
Rhodes, tel 22410 63730, fax 22410 63730
email adila@tee.gr

Samos, tel 22730 25270/23366, fax 22730 27260
email Kapnoul1@otenet.gr
Patra, tel 2610 221943, fax 2610 621076,
email abageo@otenet.gr
Komotini, tel 25310 26985, 25310 24810, 25310
25595, fax 25310 27162 email ioanniskald@yahoo.gr
Igoumenitsa, tel 26650 23493, fax 26650 24847
email hk-igoumenitsa@linos-travel.gr
Volos, tel 24210 35988, fax 24210 35989,
email paparizos.g@dsvol.gr

GHANA

367 Syngrou Ave, Athens 175 02, tel 210 948 0700-9,
fax 210 948 0710-2, telex 220550-2 STAR GR

GUATEMALA

3, 2nd Merarchias St, Piraeus 185 35, tel 210 411 2045,
fax 210 417 0742 email travel@amphitrion.gr
website www.amphitrion.gr

HUNGARY

25-29 Karneadou St, Kolonaki, Athens 106 72
tel 210 725 6800, fax 210 725 6840,
email mission.ath@kum.hu   website www.hunembassy.gr

ICELAND CONSULATE

60 Papanastasiou St, P Psyhiko 154 52, tel 210 672
6154, fax 210 677 9770

INDIA

3 Kleanthous St, Athens 106 74, tel 210 721 6227,
210 721 6481, fax 210 721 1252,
email indembassy@ath.forthnet.gr
website www.indembassyathens.gr

INDONESIA

99 Marathonodromon St, P Psyhiko 154 52

tel 210 677 4692, 210 674 2345, 210 674 6418,
fax 210 675 6955, email indath@hol.gr
website www.indonesia.gr

IRAN

16 Kallari St, P Psyhiko 154 52, tel 210 674 1937,
210 674 1436, 210 674 1783, fax 210 674 7945
email irembatn@otenet.gr website www.iranembassy.gr

IRAQ

4 Mazaraki St, P Psyhiko 154 52, tel 210 672 2330,
fax 210 671 7185, email atnemb@iraqmofamail.net

IRELAND

7 V Konstantinou St, Athens 106 74, tel 210 723 2771-2,
fax 210 729 3383, email athensembassy@dfa.ie

ISRAEL

1 Marathonodromon St, P Psyhiko 154 52
tel 210 671 9530-1, fax 210 674 9510
email info@athen.mfa.gov.il

ITALY

2 Sekeri St, Kolonaki, Athens 106 74, tel 210 361 7260-3,
fax 210 361 7330, email ambasciata.atene@esteri.it
website ambatene@esteri.it
Consular section: 135-137 El Venizelou (Thiseos), Kallithea
176 72, tel 210 953 8180/190, 210 953 1640-1,
fax 210 953 1523 email consolato.atene@esteri.it
website www.consatene@esteri.it

IVORY COAST CONSULATE

13 Lykiou St, Athens 106 56, tel 210 721 2375,
fax 210 721 6625

JAPAN

46 Ethnikis Antistaseos, Halandri 152 31
tel 210 670-9900, fax 210 670 9980

email embjapan@otenet.gr website gr.emb-japan.go.jp/

JORDAN
21 Papadiamandi St, P Psyhiko 154 52, tel 210 674 4161, fax 210 674 0578, email jor-emb1@otenet.gr

KAZAKHSTAN
122 Ymittou St, Papagou 156 69, tel 210 651 5643, fax 210 651 6362, email dpmath@otenet.gr

KOREA (South), 124 Kifissias Ave, Athens 115 26
tel 210 698 4080-2, fax 210 698 4083
email gremb@mofat.go.kr website www.mofat.go.kr/greece

KUWAIT
27 Marathonodromon St, P Psyhiko 154 52
tel 210 674 3593-5, fax 210 677 5875
email kuwemath@otenet.gr

LEBANON
6, 25th Martiou St, P Psyhiko 154 52, tel 210 675 5873, fax 210 675 5612, email grlibemb@otenet.gr

LIBERIA CONSULATE
2 Efplias St, Piraeus 185 37, tel 210 453 0807, fax 210 452 0115, email samos.island@soutos-group.gr

LIBYA
13 Vyronos St, P Psyhiko 154 52, tel 210 674 2120-1, fax 210 674 2761

LITHUANIA
49 Vas Sofias Ave, Athens 106 74
tel 210 729 4356-7, fax 210 729 4347
email info@ltambasada.gr website http://gr.mfa.lt

LUXEMBOURG
23a, Vas Sofias Ave & 2 N Vamva St, Athens 106 74
tel 210 725 6400, fax 210 725 6405,

email athenes.amb@mae.etat.lu
website www.mae.lu/grece

MALAYSIA CONSULATE
114 Alimou Ave, Argyroupolis 164 52, tel 210 991 6523,
fax 210 991 3423 email profthomas2001@yahoo.gr

MALDIVES CONSULATE
3-3a Kassandras St, Kastella, Piraeus 185 33
tel 210 422 4220, fax 210 417 3728, 210 422 4229
email crew@elvictor.com stgalanakis@elvictor.com

MALI CONSULATE
38 Kapodistriou St, Athens 104 32, tel 210 524 5520

MALTA
96 Vas Sofias Ave, Athens 115 28, tel 210 778 5138,
fax 210 778 5242, email maltaembassy.athens@gov.mt

MEXICO
14 Filikis Etairias Sq, Athens 106 73, tel 210 729 4780-2,
fax 210 729 4783 email embgrecia@sre.gob.mx

MONACO
4-6 Demokratias Ave, Neo Psyhiko 154 51
tel 210 674 4133-7, fax 210 674 7346
email mgormezano@metrad.gr

MOROCCO
5 Marathonodromou, P Psyhiko 154 52, tel 210 674 4209-10,
fax 210 674 9480, email sifamath@otenet.gr

NETHERLANDS
5-7 Vas Konstantinou Ave, Athens 106 74
tel 210 725 4900, fax 210 725 4907
email ath@minbuza.nl website www.dutchembassy.gr

NEW ZEALAND CONSULATE
76 Kifissias Ave, Ambelokipi 115 26, tel 210 692 4136,

fax 210 692 4821, email costacot@yahoo.com

NIGERIA
65 Dolianis St, Maroussi 151 24, tel 210 802 3707,
210 802 1888, 210 802 2688, fax 210 802 4208
email nigeriaembathens@yahoo.co.uk

NORWAY
23 Vas Sofias Ave, Athens 106 74, tel 210 724 6173,
fax 210 724 4989, email emb.athens@mfa.no
website www.norway.gr

PAKISTAN
6 Loukianou St, Kolonaki, Athens 106 75
tel 210 729 0122, 210 729 0214, fax 210 725 7641
email info@pak-embassy.gr; website www.pak-embassy.gr

PALESTINE DIPLOMATIC REPRESENTATION
13 Giassemion St, P Psyhiko 154 52, tel 210 672 6061,
fax 210 672 6064, email falastin@otenet.gr

PANAMA
192 Praxitelous & II Merarchias sts, Piraeus 185 35,
tel 210 428 6441-3, fax 210 428 6448-9,
email panpir5@otenet.gr

PERU
2 Semitelou St, Athens 115 28, tel 210 779 2761,
fax 210 779 2905, email lepruate@otenet.gr

PHILIPPINES
26 Antheon St, P Psyhiko 154 52, tel 210 672 1883,
210 672 1837, fax 210 672 1872,
email athenspe@otenet.gr; website athenspe.net
Honorary Consuls of Philippines:
Thessaloniki 546 22, 61 Nikis St, tel 2310 556161,
fax 2310 553602

Rhodes 851 00, 3 Australias St, PO Box 4172,
tel 22410 70590, 22410 34940, fax 22410 37401
Crete, Iraklio 712 02, 13 Kantanoleon St,
tel 2810 224834, fax 2810 226189

POLAND

22 Chrysanthemon St, P Psyhiko 154 52
tel 210 679 7700/710, fax 210 679 7711,
email info@poland-embassy.gr
website www.poland-embassy.gr

PORTUGAL

23 Vas Sofias Ave, Athens 106 74, tel 210 729 0061,
210 729 0096, 210 725 7505, 210 723 6784,
fax 210 729 0955, 210 724 5122, 210 729 0557
email embportg@otenet.gr comsecpt@otenet.gr
Consular section tel 210 729 0052

ROMANIA

7 Em Benaki St, P Psyhiko 154 52
tel 210 672 8875-6, fax 210 672 8883
email secretariat@romaniaemb.gr   website atena.mae.ro
Consular section:16 Santas St, Panorama - Thessaloniki 552
36, tel 2310 340088/340089, fax 2310 332060
email romcons@otenet.gr

RUSSIA

28 Nikiforos Lytra St, P Psyhiko 154 52, tel 210 672 6130,
210 672 5235, fax 210 674 9708, email embraf@otenet.gr
website www.greece.mid.ru
Consular section: 5 Tzavella St, 152 32 Halandri,
tel 210 674 2949, fax 210 672 9157

5 Dimosthenous St, Thessaloniki 546 24
tel 2310 257201, 2310 257666, fax 2310 257202
email thecons@hol. gr

SAUDI ARABIA
71 Marathonodromon St, P Psyhiko 154 52
tel 210 671 6911-3, fax 210 674 9833
email gremb@mofa.gov.sa

SERBIA
106 Vas Sofias Ave, Athens 115 27 tel 210 777 4344,
210 777 4355, 210 777 4430 fax 210 779 6436,
email beograd@hol.gr website www.embassyscg.gr
Consular section tel 210 747 2360, 210 747 2361

SINGAPORE CONSULATE
10-12 Kifissias Ave, Maroussi 151 25 tel 210 684 5072,
fax 210 684 7660

SLOVAKIA
4 G Seferi St, P Psyhiko 154 52 tel 210 677 1980,
210 677 1870, 210 677 1884 fax 210 677 1878,
210 677 6765 email embassy@athens.mfa.sk
website slovakembassy.gr

SLOVENIA
10 Mavili St, P Psyhiko 154 52 tel 210 677 5683-5,
fax 210 677 5680 email vat@mzz-dkp.gov.si

SOUTH AFRICA
60 Kifissias St, Maroussi 151 25, tel 210 610 6645,
fax 210 610 6640, email embassy@southafrica.gr
www.southafrica.gr

ST VINCENT & THE GRENADINES CONSULATE
Sachtouri & 8 Kantharou sts, Piraeus 185 37
tel 210 428 5725, fax 210 418 5184

SPAIN
21 Dionysiou Aeropagitou St, Athens 117 42
tel 210 921 3123, fax 210 921 3090
email emb-esp@otenet. gr; website emb-esp.gr

SRI LANKA CONSULATE
20 Kanari St, Athens 106 74, tel 210 361 4575,
fax 210 361 6287 email consulgr@otenet.gr

SWEDEN
7 Vas Konstantinou St, Athens 106 74 tel 210 726 6100,
fax 210 726 6150, email ambassaden.athen@foreign.
ministry.se website   www.swedenabroad.com/athens

SWITZERLAND
2 lasiou St, Athens 115 21, tel 210 723 0364-6,
fax 210 724 9209, email ath.vertretung@eda.admin.ch
website www.eda.admin.ch/athens
Honorary Consuls of Switzerland:
Corfu, tel 26610 43164, fax 26610 43164
Patra, tel 2610 277688, fax 2610 274688
Rhodes, tel 22410 73690/78130, fax 2241 078131
Thessaloniki, tel 2310 282214/252277,
fax 2310 252 789

SYRIA
61 Diamantidou St, P Psyhiko 154 52, tel 210 672 5577,
210 672 2324, 210 671 5713, fax 210 617 6402,
email syrembas@otenet. gr
Consular section, tel 210 672 5575

THAILAND
25 Marathonodromon St, Psyhiko 154 52
tel 210 671 0155, 210 674 9065, fax 210 674 9508,
email thaiath@otenet.gr

THE FORMER YUGOSLAV REPUBLIC OF MACEDONIA
4 Papadiamandi St, P Psyhiko 154 52, tel 210 674 9585,
210 674 9548, fax 210 674 9572,
email psichiko@otenet.gr
Consular section: 43 Tsimiski, Thessaloniki,
tel 2310 277 347-9, email dkpsolun@mfa.com.mk

TUNISIA
2 Antheon St, P Psyhiko 154 52, tel 210 671 7590,
210 674 9791, fax 210 671 3432,
email atathina@otenet.gr

TURKEY
8 Vas Georgiou II St, Athens 106 74, tel 210 726 3000,
fax 210722 9597, email info@turkishembassy.ondsl.gr

UGANDA CONSULATE
3-5 Lekka St, Athens 105 62, tel 210 325 0535

UKRAINE
2-4 Stefanou Delta St, Filothei 152 37
tel 210 680 0230, fax 210 685 4154,
email ukrembas@otenet.gr; website www.ukrembas.gr

UNITED KINGDOM
1 Ploutarchou St, Athens 106 75, tel 210 727 2600,
fax 210 727 2720, 210 727 2723
email information.athens@fco.gov.uk
website www.british-embassy.gr
Honorary Consuls of United Kingdom
email consular.athens@fco.gov.uk
Corfu, tel 26610 23457, 26610 30055,
fax 26610 37995 email corfu@british-consulate.gr
Crete, tel 2810 224012, fax 2810 243935,
email crete@british-consulate. gr
Kos, tel/fax 22420 21549, email kos@british-consulate.gr
Patra, tel 2610 277329, fax 2610 225334
Rhodes, tel 22410 22005, fax 22410 24473,
email rhodes@british-consulate.gr
Thessaloniki, tel 2310 278006, 2310 283868,
email thessaloniki@british-consulate.gr
Syros, tel 22810 82232, 22810 88922,
fax 22810 83293

Zakynthos, tel 26950 22906, 26950 48030,
26950 45386, fax 26950 23769,
email zakynthos@british-consulate.gr

URUGUAY
1c Lykavittou St, Athens 10672
tel 210 360 2635, fax 210 361 3549
email urugrec@otenet. gr

UNITED STATES AMERICA
91 Vas Sofias Ave, Athens 101 60, tel 210 721 2951
email AthensAmEmb@state.gov website usembassy.gr
Honorary Consul of USA: 43 Tsimiski St,
Thessaloniki 646 23, tel 2310 242905, fax 2310 242927

UZBEKISTAN CONSULATE
26 Pindou St, Filothei 152 37, tel 210 685 7077,
210 685 5286, fax 210 683 6285 email embuzb@otenet.gr
website www.uzbekistan.gr

VATICAN APOSTOLIC NUNCIATURE
2 Mavili St, Psyhiko 154 52, tel 210 674 3598,
fax 210 674 2849

VENEZUELA
19 Marathonodromon St, P Psyhiko 154 52
tel 210 672 9169, 210 672 1274, fax 210 672 7464
email emvenath@hol.gr   website embavenez.gr

❑ COMMUNITY ORGANISATIONS

ALBANIAN
FORUM OF ALBANIAN MIGRANTS IN GREECE, 35
Valtetsiou St, 106 81 Exarheia, tel 210 884 8173
ALBANIAN NEWSPAPER Gazeta e Athines, 10 George St,
Athens, tel 210 383 7786

AMERICAN (see USA)
ARMENIAN
ARMENIAN PUBLIC CULTURAL CENTRE, 12 Souli St,
Kallithea 117 44, Athens, tel 210 935 9982
ARMENIAN NATIONAL COMMITTEE OF GREECE,
8 Aristotelis St, Kallithea, Athens,
tel 210 957 5011, 210 957 4973
ARMENIAN YOUTH FEDERATION OF GREECE,
tel 210 957 5011
HAMAZKAYIN ARMENIAN CULTURAL AND
EDUCATIONAL UNION, tel 210 957 5011
ARMENIAN BLUE CROSS, tel 210 957 5011
ARMENIAN NATIONAL COUNCIL OF GREECE 10 Kriezi
St, Athens 105 53, tel 210 325 2067
AZAT OR (daily newspaper), 220 Sygrou Ave,
Athens 176 72, tel 210 957 5011
ARMENIKA (bi-monthly edition of Azadamart Association,
in Greek), tel 210 760 1606

ARGENTINIAN
ASSOCIATION OF ARGENTINE RESIDENTS IN GREECE
www.argentinos.gr, tel 6977 136908, 6938 262612
ASCLAYE (Latin-American and Spanish Association of
Greece) 47A Falirou St, Koukaki, tel 210 923 2204

AUSTRALIAN
AUSTRALIAN ARCHAEOLOGICAL INSTITUTE,
17 Zaharitsa St, Koukaki, tel 210 924 3256
AUSTRALIAN TRADE COMMISSION (AUSTRADE) promotes
trade and investment between Greece and Australia.
Office is at the embassy. Call 210 647 0561
or fax 210 640 1585

AUSTRIAN
AUSTRIAN ARCHAEOLOGICAL INSTITUTE, 26 Alexandras

Ave, tel 210 821 3708, oeai@hol. gr www.oeai.at
GREEK-AUSTRIAN SOCIETY, 47 Orfanidou St, Ano Patissia,
tel 210 293 2006, www.oegr.gr

BANGLADESHI
BANGLADESHI ASSOCIATION OF GREECE,
tel 6945 347703
ATHENS-BANGLA ACADEMY, 22 Evangelistrias St,
tel 6938 826695

BELGIAN
BELGIAN SCHOOL OF ATHENS, 79 Anagnostopoulou St,
210 364 7102
BELGIAN BUSINESS CLUB, tel 210 361 0120,
fax 210 361 0117
FIT (FLANDERS INTERNATIONAL TRADE),
tel 210 361 1308
AWEX (AGENCE WALLONNE A L'EXPORTATION),
tel 210 361 0125
BELGIAN ASSOCIATION OF FLEMINGS,
www.vlaamse-kring.gr

BRITISH (see UK)

BULGARIAN
ATENSKI VESTI (weekly newspaper), 10 George St,
tel 210 383 7786
KADISKA (bi-weekly newspaper), 33 Marni St,
tel 210 523 9321
KONTAKT (monthly newspaper), 4 Agiou Konstantinou St,
Omonia, tel 210 522 8319

CAMAROON
CAMAROON ASSOCIATION, tel 210 346 6441

CANADIAN
CANADIAN ARCHAEOLOGICAL INSTITUTE

7 Dion Aiginitou St, Athens, tel 210 722 3201
HELLENIC CANADIAN ASSOCIATION, tel 210 345 0211
GREEK CANADIAN ASSOCIATION, tel 210 992 6171

CHILEAN

GRECO-CHILEAN COMMERCIAL AND CULTURAL
EXCHANGE: Information about the Commercial and
Cultural Chamber can be obtained at the Embassy of Chile

CHINESE

CHINESE-GREEK FRIENDSHIP ASSOCIATION
35 Akadimias St, tel 210 364 6260,
email gr-china@otenet.gr

CUBAN

SOL DE CUBA ASSOCIATION, tel 210 964 1319

CYPRIOT

CYPRIOT CULTURAL CENTRE, 10 Irakleitou St, Kolonaki,
tel 210 364 1217
FEDERATION OF CYPRIOT ORGANISATIONS IN GREECE, 3
Kekropos St, Athens, tel 210 324 7760, www.cyprusnet.gr

CONGOLESE

REPUBLIC OF THE CONGO COMMUNITY,
tel 210 324 1361

EGYPTIAN

EL RAPTA ASSOCIATION OF EGYPTIAN WORKERS IN
GREECE, tel 210 865 9613

ESTONIA

GREEK-BALTIC CHAMBER OF COMMERCE,
34 Mitropoleos St, Thessaloniki, tel 2310 277010

ERITREAN

ERITREAN ASSOCIATION, 4 Vas Konstantinou Ave,
tel 210 701 5870

FINLAND

FINNISH SCHOOL OF PIRAEUS, tel 210 292 4803

FRENCH

AMICALE DES ALSACIENS EN GRECE, Society of Alsatians in Greece, tel /fax 210 802 9998

AMICALE FRANCAISE DES INGENIEURS ET CADRES, French society of engineers and professionals, www.amicale.gr

ASSOCIATION FRANCAISE D'ENTRAIDE, an organisation based at the French consulate in Athens that assists elderly people, tel 210 729 7700 from 10.30am to 12.30pm on Tuesdays

ASSOCIATION OF FRENCH CITIZENS ABROAD (ADFE), tel 210 600 0313

ATHENS ACCUEIL, an organisation based at the French consulate in Athens, it holds cultural events and activities, bringing together French citizens in Greece, tel 210 729 7700, from 10am till noon on Wednesdays

FRENCH-GREEK CHAMBER OF COMMERCE AND INDUSTRIES, 31 Sina St, Athens, tel 210 362 5516, email ccifhel@otenet.gr

ORGANISATIONS DE BRETONS DE L'EXTERIEUR, Organisations of Bretons Abroad, tel/fax 210 201 3773

UNION OF FRENCH CITIZENS ABROAD (UFE), tel 210 820 0700

FRENCH ARCHAEOLOGICAL SCHOOL IN ATHENS, 6 Didotou, tel 210 367 9900, fax 210 363 2101

GAMBIA

ASSOCIATION OF GAMBIAN IMMIGRANTS IN GREECE, tel 210 881 1719

GERMAN

GERMAN ARCHAEOLOGICAL INSTITUTE, 1 Phidiou St, Athens 106 78, tel 210 330 7400

GOETHE INSTITUTE, 14-16 Omirou St, Athens 106 72,
tel 210 366 1000, fax 210 364 3518,
email gi@athen. goethe. org; www.goethe.de/athens
GOETHE INSTITUTE THESSALONIKI,
66 Vas Olgas, Thessaloniki, tel 2310 889610,
fax 2310 831871, www.goethe.de/thessaloniki
GERMAN-GREEK CHAMBER OF INDUSTRY, 10-12
Dorileou, Athens 115 21, tel 210 641 9000,
fax 210 644 5175, email ahkathen@mail.ahk-gemany.de
GERMAN-GREEK CHAMBER OF INDUSTRY IN
THESSALONIKI, 50 Voulgari St, Thessaloniki 542 49,
tel 2310 327733-5, fax 2310 327737
GERMAN INFORMATION CENTRE, 24 Massalias St,
Athens 106 80, tel 210 361 2288, fax 210 361 2952

GHANAIAN
GHANAIAN ASSOCIATION, tel 6976 143586

GUINEAN
GUINEAN ASSOCIATION, tel 6972 562958

HUNGARIAN
GREEK-HUNGARIAN CULTURAL ASSOCIATION,
tel 210 921 6902

INDIAN
GREEK-INDIAN CULTURAL ASSOCIATION
16 Filellinon St, Piraeus, tel 210 418 7012

IRANIAN
CULTURAL CENTRE OF THE EMBASSY
22 Kapodistriou Ave, Maroussi, tel 210 681 8154

IRISH
GREEK-IRISH SOCIETY, tel 22990 48603,
www.greekirishsociety@hotmail.com

ITALIAN

ITALIAN SCHOOL, 18 Mitsaki St, Ano Patissia,
tel 210 228 0338
ITALIAN NEWS AGENCY 9 Kanari St, Athens,
tel 210 360 5285
ITALIAN-GREEK CHAMBER OF COMMERCE IN ATHENS,
5 Ventiri St, tel 210 721 3209, www.italia.gr
ITALIAN GREEK CHAMBER OF COMMERCE IN
THESSALONIKI, 47 Karamanlis St, tel 2310 951272
ITALIAN FOREIGN TRADE INSTITUTE IN ATHENS,
14 Vas Sofias Ave, tel 210 729 4971
ITALIAN CULTURAL INSTITUTE IN ATHENS
47 Patission St, tel 210 524 2646, www.iic.gr
ITALIAN CULTURAL INSTITUTE IN THESSALONIKI,
1 Fleming St, tel 2310 857155, www.iicsalonico.gr
SOCIETA DANTE ALIGHIERI, 18 Ayelaou St, Pangrati,
tel 210 756 1952
COAS IT (Italian Support Network), tel 210 801 7615

JAPANESE

GREEK-JAPANESE ASSOCIATION, 32 Omirou St,
Athens tel 210 363 8966
GREEK JAPANESE CHAMBER OF COMMERCE,
7 Filellinon St, Syntagma, tel 210 323 2586

JEWISH

CENTRAL BOARD OF JEWISH COMMUNITIES
IN GREECE, 36 Voulis St, Athens, tel 210 324 4315-9,
fax 210 331 3852, hhkis@hellasnet. gr www.kis.gr
JEWISH COMMUNITY HEADQUARTERS
8 Melidoni St, Athens, tel 210 325 2875, 210 325 2823,
fax 210 322 0761, email isrkath@hellasnet.gr
JEWISH CULTURAL CENTRE,
9 Vissarionos & Sina sts, 2nd floor, Athens,
tel 210 363 7092, fax 210 360 8896

COMMUNITY HEADQUARTERS/ RABBINATE/ CULTURAL
CLUB THESSALONIKI, 26 Vas Iraklio St, Thessaloniki,
tel 2310 275701, www.jct.gr
COMMUNITY HEADQUARTERS HALKIS
35 Kotsou St, Halkis
JEWISH COMMUNITY HEADQUARTERS CORFU
5 R Voulefton St, tel 26610 45650
JEWISH COMMUNITY HEADQUARTERS IOANNINA,
18B Yossef Eliya St, tel 26510 25195
JEWISH COMMUNITY HEADQUARTERS
AND CULTURAL CLUB, LARISSA,
29 Kentavron St, tel/fax 2410 532965

KENYA
KENYAN COMMUNITY ASSOCIATION, tel 210 211 4014

KOREAN
KOREAN COMMUNITY ASSOCIATION, tel 210 323 3330

MOLDOVAN
GREEK-MOLDOVAN ASSOCIATION, 24 Kaningos St,
Athens, tel 6945 484961

MOROCCO
COMMUNITY ASSOCIATION OF MORROCO,
tel 6947 878575

NETHERLANDISH
NETHERLANDS INSTITUTE IN ATHENS (Archaeological
and Cultural), 11 Makri St, Athens, tel 210 921 0760-1

NIGERIAN
NIGERIAN COMMUNITY IN GREECE, tel 210 523 6552
NIGERIAN WOMEN'S ASSOCIATION, tel 6993 151577

NORWEGIAN
THE NORDIC LIBRARY, 7 Kavalotti St, Athens 119 42,
tel 210 924 9210, fax 210 921 6487, email norlib@hol.gr

NORWEGIAN INSTITUTE IN ATHENS,
5 Tsami Karatasou St, tel 210 923 1351
NORWEGIAN SCHOOL IN ATHENS
email skolen@norskforening. net
THE NORWEGIAN ASSOCIATION IN ATHENS,
12 Taxiarhon St, Moshato, email info@norskforening.net

PAKISTANI

PAKISTANI ECONOMIC AND BUSINESS COUNCIL,
53 Eirinis St, Argiroupoli, tel 210 963 6863
AWAZ ATHENS, tel 210 520 2495
NAWA-E-WATAN, tel 210 559 5030

PHILIPPINE

KASAPI-HELLAS (Unity of Filipino Migrant Workers
in Greece), 18 Mithymnis St, Amerikis Square,
tel 210 866 4527
PHILIPPINE OVERSEAS LABOUR OFFICE, tel 210 672 8256
FILIPINO WORKERS RESOURCE CENTRE
63a Katahaki St, Neo Psyhiko, tel 210 698 3355
ABRENIAN WORKERS ASSOCIATION, tel 210 962 8095
BAGONG KAPWA KO FILIPINO SA ATHENS,
tel 210 603 6006
BICOL SARO, tel 6936 920053
BULACAN MIGRANTS ASSOCIATION, tel 210 962 8095
CANDONIANS IN ATHENS, tel 6932 590179
CANDON CITY LADIES ASSOCIATION, tel 210 622 9364
ILOCOS SUR INTERIOR ASSOCIATION, tel 210 699 7531
INTEGRATED BARANGAY OF THE PHILIPPINES
IN ATHENS, tel 210 622 9364
KATIPUNAN PHILIPPINE CULTURAL ACADEMY - KAPHILCA,
tel 210 748 0825
PHILIPPINE OVERSEAS SOCIETY, tel 210 671 5085
PUREBATS ASSOCIATION, tel 6939 449425
SAINT LUCY UNION MOVEMENT, tel 6932 179663

SAMAHAN NG MGA FILIPINO SA ATHENS,
tel 210 645 9319
TIMPUYOG LA UNION, tel 210 747 5287
TINGUIANS OF ABRA ORGANISATION,
tel 210 412 2220
TUYNIANS IN GREECE, tel 6939 652401
UNITED STO TOMAS SARANAY ASSOCIATION,
tel 6932 590179
UNITED PANGASINENSES IN GREECE, tel 210 640 1302
UNITED VISAYAS MINDANAO, tel 6936 714908
FILIPINO BOWLERS IN ATHENS, tel 6936 714908
MARINA FLISVOS, tel 6938 087367

POLISH
POLISH CLUB, tel 210 524 5926
KURIER ATENSKI, weekly newspaper
10 George St, 210 383 7786

PORTUGUESE
PORTUGUESE ASSOCIATION,
email portugueses–na–grecia@hotmail.com

ROMANIAN
SFANTUL STEFAN CEL MARE, 8 Aristotelous St,
Vathis Square, tel 210 523 1256, fax 210 981 3959
HELLENIC-ROMANIAN FRIENDSHIP ASSOCIATION TREI
IERARHI, 43 Dionissou St, tel 210 614 3773
CURIERUL ATENEI, weekly newspaper
10 George St, tel 210 383 7737
ZIARUL ROMANILOR, weekly newspaper, tel 6945 397786
ACTUALITATEA ROMANEASCA
weekly newspaper, tel 210 825 3110
EL-RO REVIEW, magazine, 82A Em Benaki St,
tel 210 330 6239
ROMANIAN LIBRARY MIHAI EMINESCU
82A Em Benaki St, tel 210 330 6239

RUSSIAN

HELLENIC RUSSIAN CHAMBER OF COMMERCE,
3 Lekkaki St, Paleo Psyhiko, tel 210 698 1127
OMONIA, weekly newspaper, 10 George St,
tel 210 383 7480
MK-ATHENS COURIER, weekly newspaper,
tel 210 984 8499

SENEGAL

SENEGAL COMMUNITY ORGANISATION,
tel 210 520 3970

SIERRA LEONEAN

SIERRA LEONEAN NATIONALS' ASSOCIATION,
tel 210 223 4753

SLOVENIAN

HELLENIC-SLOVENIAN CHAMBER OF TRADE AND
INDUSTRY, 109-111 Xanthipou, tel 210 654 0905

SPANISH

ASCLAYE (Latin-American and Spanish Association
of Greece), 47A Falirou St, Koukaki, tel 210 923 2204
SPANISH-GREEK ASSOCIATION OF ATHENS
8 Pezopoulou St, Athens, tel 210 699 3249

SOUTH AFRICAN

SOUTH AFRICANS IN GREECE, tel 6972 721122

SUDANESE

SUDANESE COMMUNITY OF GREECE, 2A Kefallinias St,
Athens, tel 210 823 2446

SWEDISH

THE SWEDISH INSTITUTE IN ATHENS, 9 Mitseon St,
Athens, tel 210 923 2102

SWISS

SWISS ARCHAEOLOGICAL SCHOOL, 4B Skaramanga St, Athens 104 33, tel 210 822 1449

TUNISIAN

TUNISIAN ASSOCIATION OF GREECE, tel 210 493 1276

UNITED KINGDOM

BRITISH GRADUATES' SOCIETY, 8A El Venizelou St, Papagou, tel 210 652 8385, fax 210 653 6069
ST ANDREW'S SOCIETY OF ATHENS, tel 22940 26443

UNITED STATES OF AMERICA

AMERICAN HELLENIC EDUCATIONAL PROGRESSIVE ASSOCIATION (AHEPA) HELLAS DISTRICT, tel 210 823 3494, 6977 941552
AHEPA, ATHENS CHAPTER HJ1, tel 210 674 4635
AHEPA GLYFADA, tel 210 964 2824
AMERICAN WOMEN'S ORGANISATION OF GREECE (AWOG) tel 210 362 4115, www.awog.gr
DAUGHTERS OF PENELOPE (HESPERUS 359 AHEPA WOMEN) 1 Grigoriou Lambraki, Ag Stefanos, tel 210 621 7668, 210 814 1137, 210 621 8866
FULBRIGHT FOUNDATION, tel 210 724 1811
HELLENIC-AMERICAN INSTITUTE INC, 36 Haritos St, Athens 106 75, tel 210 723 2706, 210 428 2383
HELLENIC-AMERICAN UNION, 22 Massalias St, Athens 106 80, tel 210 368 0000
GREEK ALUMNI OF AMERICAN UNIVERSITIES C/O Hellenic American Union, 22 Massalias, Athens 106 80, tel 210 368 0000, 210 650 3557
PROPELLER CLUB, tel 210 429 0237
REPUBLICANS ABROAD, PO Box 65023, Athens 154 10, tel 210 674 6179, fax 210 672 4753
DEMOCRATS ABROAD IN GREECE, tel 210 361 0333

HELLENIC-AMERICAN DEMOCRATIC ASSOCIATION
(HELADA) c/o Brady Kiesling, 9 Hairefontos St,
Plaka 105 58, tel/fax 210 322 7463, www.helada.org
US MILITARY RETIREE ASSOCIATION OF GREECE PCS 107,
BOX 2100, APO AE 09841,
tel 210 982 0536, 210 619 8937
YMCA, tel 210 362 6970
YWCA, tel 210 362 4291
HIOS OMOGENON SOCIETY, 1 Sgouta St,
Hios 821 00, tel 22710 44616, 22710 22747
ASSOCIATION OF REPATRIATED CRETAN
AMERICANS, 13 Findiki St, Hania 731 00,
tel 28210 90853, 28210 51290, 28210 58394
HELLENIC AMERICAN ASSOCIATION
OF THESSALY, 2 Patroklou St, Larissa 412 22,
tel 2410 2560692
DAUGHTERS OF PENELOPE (AHEPA) NAFPAKTOS,
34 Vardakoula, Nafpaktos 303 00,
tel 26340 21969, fax 28340 28495
USA GIRL SCOUTS OVERSEAS, tel 210 654 4856
USA GIRL SCOUTS OVERSEAS (southern suburbs),
tel 210 921 2949
USA BOY SCOUTS, tel 210 654 4500

VENEZUELA
GREEK-VENEZUELAN SOCIETY, tel 210 691 5410

❏ FOREIGN INSTITUTES AND SCHOOLS

MINISTRY OF EDUCATION AND RELIGIOUS AFFAIRS,
15 Mitropoleos St, Athens, tel 210 325 4221, www.ypepth.gr
**DOATAP (Hellenic National Academic Recognition and
Information Centre)** 54 Ag Constantinou St, Athens 104 37,
tel 210 528 1000, fax 210 523 9679, www.doatap.gr

BRITISH COUNCIL - ATHENS, 17 Kolonaki Sq,
tel 210 369 2333, 801 500 3692, fax 210 363 4769,
www.britishcouncil.gr
BRITISH COUNCIL - THESSALONIKI, 9 Ethnikis Amynis,
tel 2310 378300, fax 2310 241960
CERVANTES INSTITUTE, 31 Skoufa St, Athens,
tel 210 363 4117, fax 210 364 7233,
FRENCH INSTITUTE, 31 Sina St, Athens
tel 210 339 8600, fax 210 364 6873 www.ifa.gr
GOETHE INSTITUTE - ATHENS, 14 Omirou St,
Athens 106 72, tel 210 366 1000,
fax 210 364 3518, www.goethe.de/athen
GOETHE INSTITUTE - THESSALONIKI
66 Vas Olgas, Thessaloniki 546 42,
tel 2310 898610 www. goethe. de/thessaloniki
HELLENIC AMERICAN UNION (HAU), 22 Massalias St,
Kolonaki, tel 210 368 0900, fax 210 363 3174,
www.hau.gr
**HELLENIC-AFRICAN CHAMBER OF COMMERCE AND
DEVELOPMENT**, 120 Solonos St, Athens 106 81,
tel 210 381 0465, fax 210 380 5113,
info@helafrican-chamber.gr
ITALIAN CULTURAL INSTITUTE - ATHENS, 47 Patission St,
Politehnio 104 33, tel 210 524 2646/674,
fax 210 524 2714, www.iie.gr, direttore.iicatene@esteri.it
ITALIAN CULTURAL INSTITUTE - THESSALONIKI,
1 Fleming St, Thessaloniki 546 42, tel 2310 843868,
fax 2310 812057, www.iicsalonicco.gr, info@iicsalonicco.gr
LEARN GREEK ATHENS LANGUE, tel 210 331 7844
ATHENS CENTRE, 48 Arhimidou St, Athens 116 36,
tel 210 701 2268, 210 701 5242, fax 210 7018603

www.athenscentre. gr

ALEXANDER THE GREAT, Athens tel 210 821 7710,
Thessaloniki tel 2310 226318

BABEL, tel 210 964 4765, www.greeklessons-babel.gr

GREEK HOUSE, 7 Dragoumi St, Kifissia 145 62,
tel 210 808 5185/6, fax 210 808 5184,
www.greekhouse.gr

NIMA INSTITUTE 28 Papandreou St, Halandri,
tel 210 682 2736, 210 681 9309

OMILO Language & Culture, tel 210 612 2896,
fax 210 612 2706

SAPPHO SOFT, Esperidon Sq & 55 Kyprou St, Glyfada,
tel 210 898 1306

PRE-SCHOOL COTTAGE KINDERGARTEN, 74 Psaron St,
Halandri 152 32, tel 210 682 7629 www.cottage.gr

EDUCATION FOUNDATION POLKA FROELEN
tel 210 807 0566, www.polkafroelen.com,
gstathopoulos@polkafroelen.com

JACK & JILL, 2 Lomvardou, Yerakas, tel 210 661 0900,
fax 210 603 8965 www.jackjill-preschool.gr

KIFISSIA MONTESSORI SCHOOL, 5 Ellinikou Stratou St,
Kifissia 145 62, tel 210 808 0322

LE CASTELET, 18 Gortinias St, Kifissia, tel 210 808 7760

PETER PAN, 19 Vas Georgiou St, Glyfada 166 73,
tel 210 895 9654 fax 210 895 2074, www.peterpan.gr

POOH CORNER, 50 Argyroupoleos & Sampsountos, Drossia
146 71, Athens, tel 210 620 4853,
www.poohcornerkindergarten.com

SECONDARY AMERICAN COMMUNITY SCHOOLS OF ATHENS
(ACS Athens), 129 Agias Paraskevis St, Halandri 152 34,
tel 210 639 3200, fax 210 639 0051, www.acs.gr

ATHENS COLLEGE-PSYHIKO COLLEGE
15 Stef Delta St, P Psyhiko, tel 210 679 810,
fax 210 674 8457 www.haef.gr

BYRON COLLEGE, 7 Filolaou St, Gargitos, Yerakas 153 44,
tel 210 604 7722-5, fax 210 604 8542, www.byroncollege.gr
CAMPION SCHOOL PALLINI, Ag Ioulianis, Pallini 153 44,
tel 210 607 1850, fax 210 607 1750, www.campion.edu.gr
COSTEAS-GEITONAS SCHOOL, Pallini 153 51, Attica,
tel 210 603 0411-7, fax 210 603 0570, www.cgs.gr
ELLINOGERMANIKI AGOGI (German) 25 Doukissis Plakentias
St, Halandri 152 34, tel 210 817 6700,
fax 210 603 2554, www.ellinikogermaniki.gr
FRENCH-GREEK SCHOOL (ST PAUL)
36 Harilaou Trikoupi St, Piraeus 185 36, tel 210 451 1954,
fax 210 453 7721, www.saintpaul.gr
GEITONAS SCHOOL, Vari 166 02, Attica,
tel 210 965 6200/10, fax 210 965-5920,
www.geitonas-school.gr
GERMAN SCHOOL, Athens Dimokritou & Ziridi sts, Maroussi
151 23, tel 210 619 9261, fax 210 619 9267,
www.dsathen.edu.gr
GERMAN SCHOOL Thessaloniki PO Box 51,
Phinikas, Thessaloniki 551 02, tel 2310 475900-2,
fax 2310 476232, www.dst.gr
GREEK-GERMAN SCHOOL, 9 D Vernardou
and 25 Martiou St, Vrilissia 152 35, tel 210 682-0566,
tel/fax 210 684 4063
ITALIAN SCHOOL 18 Mitsaki St, Athens 111 41,
tel 210 228 0338, fax 210 201 7628, scitalat@otenet.gr
JEWISH ELEMENTARY SCHOOL, in the suburb of Paleo
Psyhiko
JEWISH ELEMENTARY SCHOOL, 17 Fleming St, Thessaloniki
MANTA-PAPADATOU (German), 75 Amaroussiou-Halandriou,
Maroussi 151 25, tel 210 682 5447
MUNTING YAYON FILIPINO SCHOOL
18 Mithymnis St, Amerikis Square, tel 210 866 4527

PINEWOOD SCHOOLS OF THESSALONIKI, PO Box 210 01,
Pylea 555 10, Thessaloniki, tel 2310 301 221,
fax 2310 323196, www.pinewood.gr
POLISH COMMUNITY SCHOOL, 19 Navarinou St, Holargos,
tel 210 653 8204
ST CATHERINE'S BRITISH EMBASSY SCHOOL,
73 Sof Venizelou St, Lykovrissi 141 23, tel 210 282
9750/1, fax 210 282 6415 www.stcatherines.gr
ST LAWRENCE COLLEGE, Anemon Street, Loutsa-Kouke Area,
Koropi, Attikis tel 210 891 7000, fax 210 891 7010,
www.st-lawrence.gr
THE INTERNATIONAL SCHOOL OF GREECE, Artemidos &
Xenias sts, Kefalari, Kifissia 145 10, tel 210 623 3888,
fax 210623 3160, www.isa.edu.gr
**HIGHER EDUCATION ALBA (ATHENS LABORATORY OF
BUSINESS ADMINISTRATION)**, Athinas Ave & 2 Areos St,
Vouliagmeni, tel 210 896 4531, fax 210 896 4737,
www.alba.edu.gr
**ALPINE CENTRE FOR HOTEL AND TOURISM MANAGEMENT
STUDIES**, 70 Poseidonas Ave, Glyfada 166 75, tel 210 898
3022, fax 210 898 1189, www.alpine.edu.gr
AMERICAN COLLEGE OF GREECE (Pierce College, Deree
College, Junior College), 6 Gravias St,
Agia Paraskevi 153 42, tel 210 600 9800-9,
fax 210 600 9819, www.acg.edu.gr
AMERICAN COLLEGE OF THESSALONIKI (ANATOLIA),
PO Box 210 21, Pylea 555 10, Thessaloniki,
tel 2310 398356, fax 2310 301 076, www.act.edu.act
AMERICAN FARM SCHOOL, PO Box 23,
Thessaloniki 551 02, tel 2310 492 819,
info@afs.edu.gr; website www.afs.edu.gr
**ATHENS INSTITUTE OF TECHNOLOGY MEDICINE, SCIENCE
& LAW**, 95 Alexandras Avenue, Athens 114 74,

tel 210 6424342, 210 640 0383, fax 210 646 1224, www.athensinstitute-ac.gr

BUSINESS STUDIES, 4 Dimitressas St, Athens 115 28, tel 210 725 3783, www.bca.gr

CHEF D'OEUVRE, 20 Heiden St, Athens 104 34, tel 210 823 7758, 210 823 1935, www.chefdoeuvre.gr

CITY Liberal Studies, 13 Tsimiski St, Thessaloniki 546 24, tel 2310 224186, fax 2310 287564 www.city.academic.gr

EUROPEAN UNIVERSITY, 2 Vas Konstantinou Ave, 1 Stadiou Sq, Kalimarmaro, Athens 116 35, tel 210 756 0040, fax 210 752 2640, www.euruni.edu

INDEPENDENT SCIENCE & TECHNOLOGY STUDIES (IST), 72 Piraeus St, Moschato 183 46, tel 800 11 93000, 210 482 2222 www.ist.edu.gr

INTERNATIONAL MANAGEMENT STUDIES 85 Denokratous St, Athens 115 21, tel 210 723 0814, 210 725 8773 fax 210 725 8773, www.imstudies.gr

LE MONDE, 60 Halkokondili St, Athens, tel 210 523 0530, 210 523 0442, www.lemonde.edu.gr

MEDITERRANEAN COLLEGE, 107 Patission St, Athens, tel 210 889 9600, 800-11-939393, fax 210 8899610, mediterranean@medecs.gr, www.medecs.com

METROPOLITAN COLLEGE OF ARTS & SCIENCES, 74 Sorrou St, Maroussi 151 25, tel 210 619 9891, www.athensmetropolitancollege.gr

NEW YORK COLLEGE, 38 Amalias Ave, Athens 105 58, tel 210 322 5961, email nycath@nyc.gr, www.nyc.gr

NORTH COLLEGE, 7 Kountouriotou St, Thessaloniki 546 25, tel 2310-464410, fax 2310 465665, www.north.edu.gr

SBS STUDIES OF BUSINESS SCIENCE, 38 Amalia St, Athens 105 58, tel 210 322 5961-2, website www.sbs.gr

THE AMERICAN UNIVERSITY OF ATHENS, Kifisias & 4 Sohou St, Neo Psyhiko, Athens 115 25, tel 210 725 9301,

210 725 9302, 210 647 0000, fax 210 725 9304,
www.southeastern.edu.gr
TRINITY INTERNATIONAL HOSPITALITY STUDIES
tel 28970 26200, fax 28970 26203, www.trinity.edu.gr
UNIVERSITY OF INDIANAPOLIS, 9 Ipitou St, Syntagma Sq,
Athens 105 57, tel 210 323 6647, fax 210 324 8502,
www.uindy.gr

❏ MISCELLANEOUS ORGANISATIONS

12 STEP (Co-Dependents Anonymous), tel 210 865 4381
AL-ANON, tel 210 380 8582
ALCOHOLICS ANONYMOUS ATHENS, tel 210 522 0416
ALCOHOLICS ANONYMOUS THESSALONIKI
tel 6974 609533
A MATHS AND PHYSICS GROUP COMMUNITY
tel 6947 884001
ATHENS HOCKEY CLUB, tel 6942 404066, 210 617 8030,
amavridis@panafonet.gr
ATHENS SINGERS, tel 210 653 8021, 6937 229418,
6946 068724
ATHENS SPARTANS RUGBY CLUB, tel 210 895 1484
BOY SCOUTS, tel 210 723 2165
FAMILIES ANONYMOUS, tel 210 894 4503
DRUG PROBLEM, family anonymous English-speaking support,
tel 210 894 4503, 6977 774007
FRIENDLY BIRTHS, tel 210 261 6155, 6946 622891
FRIENDS CORNER ENGLISH SPEAKING PLAYGROUP,
tel 210 962 2140, www.friendscorner.gr
HANIA AA, tel 28250 22319/6947 966389
HASH HOUSE HARRIERS - ATHENS, tel 210 213 8611,
www.dalidahxxl@yahoo.co.uk
HASH HOUSE HARRIERS - THESSALONIKI

tel 2310 505123, benjamin.atkins@ear.eu.int
LA LECHE LEAGUE, tel 210 622 9885
NEWCOMERS BY THE SEA, tel 210 899 5061
OVEREATERS ANONYMOUS, tel 210 346 2800
PEDESTRIANS' RIGHTS ASSOCIATION
tel 210 689 3697, www.pezh.gr
THE RAINBOW CHOIR, a Cretan international group of
singers, tel 28410 27444, email ingapediaditi@hotmail.com
RUGBY, tel 6948 884405 www.athensrugby.com
THE SOLOMON SINGERS, tel 6932 737916,
email ksolomon@ath. forthnet. gr
**THE THESSALONIKI ORGANISATION FOR WOMEN'S
EMPLOYMENT AND RESOURCES (TOWER),**
www.tower4women.gr
THESSALONIKI RUGBY CLUB, tel 6977 507218
YOUTH RUGBY, on grass tel 6977 681681, 6972 361779

❏ PLACES OF WORSHIP

ANGLICAN

see www.athensanglicans.com or send an email to
anglican@otenet.gr
ST PAUL'S CHURCH, 29 Filellinon St, tel 210 721 4906
ST PETER'S CHURCH (at St Catherine's British Embassy
School), 73 Sof Venizelou, Lykovrissi, tel 210 614 8198
ALL SAINTS CHURCH (in the Roman Catholic Church), corner
of Alkyonidon Ave and Daphni sts, Voula, tel 210 721 4906
ST JUDE CHURCH, the Upper Room, Batsi, Andros,
tel 22820 41102
HANIA, Kefala, Apokoronou, Crete, tel 28250 22345
HOLY TRINITY CHURCH, Corfu Town, tel 26610 31467
NAFPLIO (in the Roman Catholic Church) tel 27520 59139
ST ANDREW'S CHURCH, Patras, Ag Andreou St,

tel 27520 59139
THESSALONIKI (in the German Evangelical Church),
13 Paleon Patron Germanou, tel 2310 426756

ARMENIAN

ARMENIAN ORTHODOX PRELACY, 10 Kriezi St, Athens,
tel 210 325 2067
ST GARABET ORTHODOX CHURCH, 4 Praksagora St,
Neos Kosmos, tel 210 921 5452
ST AGOP ORTHODOX CHURCH, Armenikis Orthodoxis
Ekklisias, 12 Florinis St, Paleia Kokkinia, tel 210 491 5823
ARMENIAN ORTHODOX CHURCH VIRGIN MARY,
4 Dialeti, Thessaloniki 546 21, tel 2310 275352
HOLY CROSS ARMENIAN ORTHODOX CHURCH,
4 Ioakim Sgourou St, Kavala 653 02
ARMENIAN ORTHODOX CHURCH, 54 Agiou Eleftheriou,
Xanthi 671 00
ST KRIKOR LUSAVORICH ORTHODOX CHURCH,
52 Vas Georgiou St, Komotini 691 00, tel 25310 27451
ST GARABET ORTHODOX CHURCH, 54 An Thrakis St,
Alexandroupolis 681 00, tel 25510 36683
ST GEORGE ORTHODOX CHURCH, Patriarchou Dionisiou,
Didimotiho 683 00, tel 25310 27451

BAPTIST

BIBLE BAPTIST CHURCH, 14 Kourtesi St, Halandri,
tel 210 601 2054
TRINITY INTERNATIONAL BAPTIST CHURCH,
39 Heldreich St, Neos Kosmos, tel 210 962 8471
CHURCH OF CHRIST, 28 Tsaldaris (Pireos) St,
Omonia Square, tel 210 523 7030, 10 Evrou, Ambelokipi,
tel 210 779 4840

ETHIOPIAN EVANGELICAL

ETHIOPIAN EVANGELICAL CHRISTIAN FELLOWSHIP,

58 Pergamou St, Attikis tel 210 865-3013,
(place of worship: 41 Sofokleous St, 3rd floor, Athens)

JEWISH

A SEPHARDIC BETH SHALOM SYNAGOGUE, 5 Melidoni St, Thissio, tel 210 325 2773, 210 324 4314-8
A ROMANIOTE SYNAGOGUE, 8 Melidoni St, Thissio (open primarily on High Holidays)
A MONASTIRIOTON SYNAGOGUE, 35 Syngrou St, Thessaloniki, tel 2310 524968 (open primarily on High Holidays)
A YAD LEZICARON SYNAGOGUE, 24 Vassileos Irakliou St, Thessaloniki, tel 2310 223231
SYNAGOGUE, 35 Kotsou St, Halkis, tel 22210 80690
GRECA SYNAGOGUE, Velissariou St, Corfu
ETZ HAYYIM SYNAGOGUE, Parodos Kondilaki, Hania, Crete, tel 28210 86286, email dori@grecian.net
www.etz-hayyim-hania.org
ROMANIOTE SYNAGOGUE, 16 Ioustinianou St (in the Walled City), Ioannina
ETZ HAYYIM SYNAGOGUE, Kentavron & 89 Kiprou St, Larissa
SYNAGOGUE, Dosiadou & Simou St, Rhodes
SYNAGOGUE, 15 Athanassiou Diakou St, Trikala
SYNAGOGUE, Merarchias St (in the Barboula Jewish quarter), Veria
SYNAGOGUE, Xenophontos & Moisseos sts, Volos

ORTHODOX

METROPOLIS (Cathedral) Mitropoleos St, tel 210 322 1308
ST SPIRIDON, 13 Eratoshenous, Pangrati
AGIA TRIADA (RUSSIAN ORTHODOX), 21 Filellinon St

PENTECOSTAL

HELLENIC INTERNATIONAL CHRISTIAN FELLOWSHIP,

36 Aristidou Oikonomou St, Kato Patissia, tel 210 854 0513
NIGERIAN CHURCH (CHRISTIAN PENTACOST MISSION
INTERNATIONAL), 41 Sofokleous St, Omonia, tel 6944
953458, Sunday 10am worship, Pastor Jude Uzor

GERMAN EVANGELICAL

EVANGELISCHE KIRCHE DEUTSCHER SPRACHE,
66 Sina St, Athens 106 72, tel 210 361 2713

SWEDISH EVANGELICAL
SCANDINAVIAN CHURCH

SCANDINAVIAN CHURCH, 282 Akti Themistokleous, Piraeus
185 10, tel 210 451 6564

PROTESTANT (non-denominational)

ST ANDREW'S INTERNATIONAL PROTESTANT CHURCH,
tel 210 645 2583

ROMAN CATHOLIC

ST DENIS' ROMAN CATHOLIC CATHEDRAL
Sina and 2-4 Panepistimiou St, tel 210 362 3603
HOLY APOSTLES CHURCH, 77 Alkyonidos &
1 Dafnis, Voula, tel 210 895 8694
FRENCH-SPEAKING COMMUNITY, Carmelites Chapel,
16, 25th Martiou St, Paleo Iraklio, tel 210 281 1667
SISTERS OF ST JOSEPH, 10 Harilaou Trikoupi St,
tel 210 360 0190
IEROS NAOS CHRISTOU SOTIROS, 28 Mihail Voda
(near Omonia), tel 210 883 5911
ST PAUL'S CATHOLIC CHURCH, 4 Kokkinaki St, Kifissia,
tel 210 801 2526
CATHOLIC CHURCH OF ST JOHN THE BAPTIST,
11 Papanastasiou St, Paleo Psyhiko, tel 210 671 1410
DEUTSCHSPRACHIGE KATHOLISCHE GEMEINDE ST
MICHAEL, 10 Ekali St, Kifissia 106 72, tel 210 625 2647,

www.dkgathen.com
POLISH CHURCH, 28 Mihail Voda, Aharnon, tel 210 883 5911
SEVENTH-DAY ADVENTIST,
18 Keramikou St (near Omonia Sq), tel 210 522 4962
OTHER CHURCHES
THE REDEEMED CHRISTIAN CHURCH OF GOD, HOUSE
OF PRAYER PARISH, ATHENS, GREECE, 41 Sofokleous
Street, 5th floor, Omonia, Athens tel/fax 210 324 4940
CHURCH SCIENCE, FIRST CHURCH OF CHRIST, SCIENTIST
7a Vissarionos St (off Omirou), Kolonaki, tel 210 363 0641
GLYFADA CHRISTIAN CENTRE, 117 Saki Karagiorga St,
Ano Glyfada, tel 210 965 1346
AGAPE FILIPINO CHRISTIAN FELLOWSHIP, 5 Timoleontos &
Defner St, Mets 116 38, Athens, tel/fax 210 722-0551,
email afcf@hotmail.com
BREAD OF LIFE CHRISTIAN FELLOWSHIP, 19 Folegandrou St,
Athens, tel 6937 933790
CATHOLIC CHARISMATIC RENEWAL MOVEMENT,
11 Thironos St, Kaisariani 161 21, Athens, tel 210 684 6343
CATHOLIC UNION OF FILIPINOS IN ATHENS (CUFA),
5 Xenias St, Platia Mavili, Ambelokipi, Athens,
tel 6947 230022
COUPLES FOR CHRIST FAMILY RENEWAL MINISTRY,
3 Fokidos St, Athens, 210 775 2806
GAWAD KALINGA, tel 6944 178796, 6944 983282
EL SHADDAI GROUP (DWXI Prayer Partner Foundation Int'l -
Piraeus) 2 Kokkini St, Kosmos 117 43, Athens,
tel 210 894 5566, 210 729 3991
FILIPINO CHRISTIAN FELLOWSHIP OF ATHENS (FCFA),
19 Ahaias St, Ambelokipi 115 26, Athens, tel 210 807 4622
GLOBAL HEART MISSION INC, 80 Dimitrakopoulos St,
Kolonaki 11741, Athens, tel 6938 006296

IGLESIA NI KRISTO, 97 Marathonodromou St,
Paleo Psyhico, Athens 154 52, tel 210 884 2613, 8 Aberof
Argiropouli St, Vouliagmenis, Athens, 210 677 0730
INTERNATIONAL CHRISTIAN MINISTRIES, 10 Kirras St,
Ambelokipi, Athens, or 25 Ahaias St, Ambelokipi (1st floor),
Athens 11523, tel 6939 243413
INTERCONTINENT FULL GOSPEL MINISTRIES,
tel 6932 679719
MIRACULOUS MEDAL CENTRE, 9a Sorovits St,
Patission 112 52, Athens, tel 210 864 1193
LEGION OF MARY, 22 Fivis St, Glyfada 166 74, Athens,
tel 6944 531006, 6944 774931
MORE THAN CONQUERORS IN CHRIST FELLOWSHIP,
41 Sofokleous St (4th floor), Athens, tel 210 899 3149
RIVER OF LIFE INTERNATIONAL FELLOWSHIP, 1 Maiandrou
St, Ilissia 115 28, Athens, tel 210 722 4395
PASTORAL GROUP, 43 Antheon St, Paleo Psyhiko 154 52,
Athens, tel 210 674 8435
PHILIPPINE BENEVOLENT MISSIONARIES ASSOCIATION
(PBMA), 109-111 Sevastopouleos St, Ambelokipi 11526,
Athens, tel 6946 515987
SERVANTS OF CHRIST FELLOWSHIP, 10 Paraschou St,
Athens 11476, tel 210 645 9214
SERVANT COMMUNITIES, 17-19 Kritonos St,
Athens 116 34, tel 210 723 7254

JEHOVAH'S WITNESSES

77 Kifissias Ave, Maroussi, tel 210 619 7630

❏ ATHLETIC ORGANISATIONS

ATHENIANS HOCKEY CLUB, tel 210 617 8030
ATHENS HORSE RIDING ASSOCIATION,
tel 210 681 2506

ATHENS TENNIS CLUB, tel 210 923 2872
ATTICA SAILING SCHOOL, tel 210 981 8740
ATTICA SPRINGBOK RUGBY CLUB, tel 6978 959852
FILOTHEI TENNIS CLUB, tel 210 681 2557
HELLENIC GOLD FEDERATION, tel 210 894 1933
GREEK BOXING FEDERATION, tel 210 867 0834
GREEK FEDERATION FOR BODY-BUILDING,
tel 210 862 2706
HELLENIC AERONAUTICAL AND AIRSPORTS FEDERATION
tel 210 964 9788, 210 964 9876
HELLENIC ARCHERY FEDERATION, tel 210 640 0186
HELLENIC AMATEUR BASEBALL FEDERATION
www.baseballgreece.com info@baseballgreece.com
HELLENIC FOOTBALL FEDERATION, tel 210 930 6000
HELLENIC BASKETBALL FEDERATION, tel 210 681 3066
HELLENIC CYCLING FEDERATION, tel 210 285 4042
HELLENIC FEDERATION OF UNDERWATER ACTIVITIES,
tel 210 981 9961
HELLENIC FENCING ASSOCIATION, tel 210 363 9781
HELLENIC HANDBALL ASSOCIATION, tel 210 884 1841
HELLENIC OFFSHORE RACING CLUB (sailing),
tel 210 412 3357
HELLENIC ROWING ASSOCIATION, tel 210 411 8011
HELLENIC SKI ASSOCIATION, tel 210 323 0182
HELLENIC SWIMMING FEDERATION, tel 210 985 1020
HELLENIC TABLE TENNIS, tel 210 522 7103
HELLENIC TENNIS FEDERATION, tel 210 756 3313
HELLENIC VOLLEYBALL FEDERATION, tel 210 922 2137
HELLENIC WATER-SKIING ASSOCIATION,
tel 210 994 4334
HELLENIC WEIGHTLIFTING ASSOCIATION,
tel 210 923 1683
HELLENIC YACHTING FEDERATION, tel 210 940 4828

KARATE SCHOOL (Goju Ryo), tel 210 976 1103
MOUNTAIN CLIMBING CLUBS' FEDERATION,
tel 210 323 8706
POLITIA TENNIS CLUB, tel 210 620 2144
TATOI HORSE RIDING CLUB, tel 210 681 2506
WATER SKIING VOULIAGMENI NAUTICAL CLUB,
tel 210 896 2416
YACHT CLUB OF GREECE, tel 210 417 9730

❏ HOSPITALS

ATHENS
Agia Eleni 21 D Soutsou, Athens 115 21
tel 210 641 0445-7
Agia Olga 3-5 Agias Olgas, N Ionia 143 88
tel 210 277 6612-7, 210 279 9265-7
Agia Varvara 1 Dodecanissou, Agia Varvara 123 51
tel 210 530 1100
Agii Anargyri 145 Kaliftaki, N Kifissia,
145 64 tel 210 238 8789
Agios Savvas 171 Alexandras, Athens 115 22
tel 210 640 9000
Alexandras (Maternity) 80 Vas Sofias, Athens 115 28
tel 210 338 1100
Amalia Fleming 14, 25 Martiou, Melissia 151 27
tel 210 613 1841
Andreas Syngkros (Dermatology) 5 Dragoumi,
Athens 161 21 tel 210 726 5000, 210 726 5100
Elena Venizelos (Maternity) 2 Elenas Venizelou Sq, Athens
106 72 tel 210 640 2000
Elpis 7 Dimitsanas, Athens 115 22 tel 210 649 4000
Errikos Dynan 107 Mesogion, Athens 115 26
tel 210 697 2000

Evangelismos 45-47 Ipsilantou, Athens 106 75
tel 210 720 1000
First IKA hospital Athens Zaimi, Melissia 151 27
tel 210 613 8460
Ippokratio 114 Vas Sofias, Athens 115 27
tel 210 748 3770 (24 lines)
KAT 2 Nikis, Kifissia 145 61 tel 210 628 0000
Korgialenio-Benakio (Erythros Stavros)
1 Athanasaki, Athens 115 26 tel 210 641 4000
Laiko 17 Agiou Thoma, Athens 115 27, tel 210 745 6000
Ophtalmiatrio Athinon (Ophthalmological)
26 El Venizelou, Athens 106 72, tel 210 362 3191/2
Paedon, Pan & Aglaias Kyriakou (Children) Thivon &
Livadias sts, Goudi 115 27 tel 210 772 6000
Paedon, Agia Sofia (Children) Thivon &
Papadiamantopoulou sts, Goudi 115 27, tel 210 746 7000
Paedon, Pendeli (Children) 2 Ippokratous, P Pendeli 152 35
tel 210 803 6200
Pammakaristos 43 Iakovaton, Athens 111 44
tel 210 228 4851-5
Patission Prefectural General Hospital 15-17 Halkidos,
Athens 111 43 tel 210 250 2140, 210 253 0935
Polikliniki 3 Piraeus, Athens 105 52, tel 210 527 6000
Sismanoglio 1 Sismanoglio, Maroussi 151 26
tel 210 803 9911
Sotiria 152 Mesogion, Athens 115 27, tel 210 777 8611-9
Thriasio Y Yennimata Ave, Magoula 196 00
tel 210 553 4200, 210 555 1501-8
Yiorgos Yennimatas 154 Mesogion, Athens
tel 210 776 8000

Psychiatric Hospitals

Athens Psychiatric Clinic 374 Athinon, Haidari 124 62
tel 210 538 8899

Children's Psychiatric clinic Crossroads, Rafina 190 09
tel 22940 77777
Dromokaitio 343 Iera Odos, Haidari
124 61 tel 210 540 4100

PIRAEUS & south suburbs

Agios Panteleimon 3 Dim Mandouvalou, Piraeus
tel 210 425 2850
Attikon 1 Rimini, Haidari tel 210 583 1000
Asklipiio, 1 Vas Pavlou, Voula 166 73, tel 210 892 4444
Metaxa 51 Botasi, Piraeus 185 37 tel 210 428 5000-11,
210 428 4444
Onasio (Cardiological) 356 Syngrou, Kallithea 176 74
tel 210 949 3000
Tzanio Afendouli & Zanni sts, Piraeus, tel 210 451 9411

UNIVERSITY HOSPITALS

Areteon, 76 Vas Sofias, Athens 115 28, tel 210 728 6000
Eginitio, 72 Vas Sofias, Athens 115 28, tel 210 728 9500

ARMY, NAVY & AIRFORCE HOSPITALS

251 Airforce Hospital, Mesogion, Katehaki
tel 210 746 3399
401 Army Hospital, 138 Mesogion, Katehaki
tel 210 749 4000
417 Nimits Hospital, 12 Monis Petraki, Athens 115 21
tel 210 728 8001
Navy Hospital Athens, 70 Dinokratous, tel 210 721 6451

AEGEAN ISLANDS

Aegina Medical Centre,	tel 22970 22222
Agathonisi Medical Centre,	tel 22470 29049
Agios Efstratios Medical Centre,	tel 22540 93222
Alonissos Medical Centre,	tel 24240 65208
Amorgos Medical Centre,	tel 22850 71207

Anafi Medical Centre,	tel 22860 61215
Andiparos Medical Centre,	tel 22840 61219
Andros Medical Centre,	tel 22820 22222
Angistri Medical Centre,	tel 22970 91111
Astypalea Medical Centre,	tel 22430 61222
Donousa Medical Centre,	tel 22850 51506
Elafonissos Medical Centre,	tel 27340 61294
Folegandros Medical Centre,	tel 22860 41222
Fourni Medical Centre,	tel 22750 51202
Halki Medical Centre,	tel 22460 45206
Hios Prefectural General Hospital,	tel 22710 44303/5
Hydra Medical Centre,	tel 22980 52420
Ikaria, Agios Kirykos Prefectural General Hospital,	tel 22750 22330
Inousses Medical Centre,	tel 22710 55300
Ios Medical Centre,	tel 22860 91227
Iraklia Medical Centre,	tel 22850 71388
Kalymnos General Hospital,	tel 22430 28851
Karpathos Medical Centre,	tel 22450 22228
Kassos Medical Centre,	tel 22450 41333
Kastelorizo Medical Centre,	tel 22460 49267
Kimolos Medical Centre,	tel 22870 51222
Kythnos Medical Centre,	tel 22810 31202
Kos General Hospital,	tel 22420 22300, 23423
Koufonissia Medical Centre,	tel 22850 71370
Leros General Hospital,	tel 22470 23251
Lesvos, Bostanio Prefectural General Hospital, Mytillini	tel 22510 57700
Limnos, Mirina General Hospital,	tel 22540 82000
Lipsi Medical Centre,	tel 22470 41204
Megisti Medical Centre,	tel 22460 49267
Milos Medical Centre,	tel 22870 22700-2
Mykonos Medical Centre,	tel 22890 23994

Naxos Medical Centre,	tel 22850 23333
Nisyros Medical Centre,	tel 22420 31217
Paros Medical Centre,	tel 22840 22500-2
Patmos Medical Centre,	tel 22470 31211
Poros Medical Centre,	tel 22980 22600/42222
Psara Medical Centre,	tel 22740 61277
Rhodes, Andreas Papandreou Prefectural General Hospital,	tel 22410 80000
Salamina Medical Centre,	tel 210 465 1888
Samos, Agios Pandeleimon Prefectural General Hospital,	tel 22730 83100
Samothraki Medical Centre,	tel 25510 41217
Santorini Medical Centre,	tel 22860 23333
Schinousa Medical Centre,	tel 22850 71385
Serifos Medical Centre,	tel 22810 51202
Sifnos Medical Centre,	tel 22840 31315
Sikinos Medical Centre,	tel 22860 51211
Skiathos Medical Centre,	tel 24270 22222
Skopelos Medical Centre,	tel 24240 22222
Skyros Medical Centre,	tel 22220 92222
Spetses Medical Centre,	tel 22980 72472
Symi Medical Centre,	tel 22460 70090
Syros Prefectural General Hospital,	tel 22810 96500/30
Thassos Medical Centre,	tel 25930 71100/2
Tilos Medical Centre,	tel 22460 44219
Tinos Medical Centre,	tel 22830 22210

CRETE

Agios Nikolaos Prefectural General Hospital,	tel 28410 66000
Hania, Agios Georgios Prefectural General Hospital,	tel 28210 22000

Ierapetra Prefectural General Hospital, tel 28420 90222
Iraklio, Venizelio General Hospital, tel 2810 368000
Iraklio University General Hospital, tel 2810 392111
Rethymno Prefectural General Hospital, tel 28310 87100
Sitia Prefectural General Hospital, tel 28430 24311

IONIAN ISLANDS

Ithaka Medical Centre, tel 26740 32222
Kefalonia, Argostoli Prefectural
General Hospital, tel 26710 24641-6
Kefalonia, Matzavinata Prefectural
General Hospital, Lyxouri tel 26710 92222
Kerkyra (Corfu) Prefectural
General Hospital, tel 26610 88200
Lefkada Prefectural General Hospital, tel 26450 25371
Paxi Medical Centre, tel 26620 31466
Zakynthos Prefectural General Hospital, tel 26950 59100

MAINLAND GREECE

AHAIA

Aegio Prefectural General Hospital, tel 26910 22222
Kalavryta Prefectural General Hospital, tel 26920 22226
Patra, Agios Andreas Prefectural
General Hospital, tel 2610 227000
Patra Prefectural General
Paediatrics Hospital, tel 2610 622222
Rio University General Hospital, tel 2610 999111

AKARNANIA & ETOLIA

Agrinio Prefectural General Hospital, tel 26410 57333
Mesolongi Prefectural General Hospital, tel 26310 57100

ARGOLIDA

Argos Hospital, tel 27510 64290
Nafplio Hospital, tel 27520 98100

ARKADIA
Tripoli, Panarkadiko Hospital,   tel 2710 371700

ARTA
Arta Prefectural General Hospital,   tel 26810 22222

DRAMA
Drama Prefectural General Hospital,   tel 25210 23351

EVIA
Halkida Prefectural General Hospital,   tel 22210 35100
Karystos Prefectural General Hospital,   tel 22240 24004
Kymi Prefectural General Hospital,   tel 22220 22222

EVRITANIA
Karpenissi Prefectural General Hospital,   tel 22370 80680

EVROS
Alexandroupolis Prefectural
General Hospital,   tel 25510 74000
Didymotiho Prefectural General Hospital,   tel 25530 44100

FLORINA
Florina Prefectural General Hospital,   tel 23850 22555

FOKIDA
Amfissa Prefectural General Hospital,   tel 22650 28888

FTHIOTIDA
Lamia Prefectural General Hospital,   tel 22310 30111

GREVENA
Grevena Prefectural General Hospital,   tel 24620 74400

HALKIDIKI
Polygyros Prefectural General Hospital,   tel 23710 20101

ILIA
Amaliada Prefectural General Hospital,   tel 26220 22222

Krestena Prefectural General Hospital,   tel 26250 23500
Pyrgos Prefectural General Hospital,   tel 26210 82300

IMATHIA

Naoussa Prefectural General Hospital,   tel 23320 22200
Veria Prefectural General Hospital,   tel 23310 22082

IOANNINA

Ioannina, Hatzikosta Prefectural
General Hospital,   tel 26510 80111
Ioannina University General Hospital,   tel 26510 99111

KAVALA

Kavala Prefectural General Hospital,   tel 2510 292000

KARDITSA

Karditsa Prefectural General Hospital   tel 24410 65555

KASTORIA

Kastoria Prefectural General Hospital,   tel 24670 55600

KILKIS

Goumenissa Prefectural General Hospital,   tel 23430 42222
Kilkis Prefectural General Hospital,   tel 23410 38400

KORINTHIA

Corinth Prefectural General Hospital,   tel 27410 25711

KOZANI

Kozani Prefectural General Hospital,   tel 24610 67600
Ptolemaida Bodosakio Hospital,   tel 24630 54000

LAKONIA

Molai Prefectural General Hospital,   tel 27320 22922
Sparta Prefectural General Hospital,   tel 27310 28671

LARISSA

Larissa Prefectural General Hospital,   tel 2410 230031
Larissa University General Hospital,   tel 2410 617000

MAGNISIA
Volos Prefectural General Hospital,   tel 24210 94200

MESSINIA
Kalamata Prefectural General Hospital,   tel 27210 46000
Kyparissia Prefectural General Hospital, tel 27610 24051-3

PELLI
Edessa Prefectural General Hospital,   tel 23810 27442
Yiannitsa Prefectural General Hospital,   tel 23820 56200

PIERIA
Katerini Prefectural General Hospital,   tel 23510 57200

PREVEZA
Preveza Prefectural General Hospital,   tel 26820 46200

RODOPI
Komotini Prefectural General Hospital,   tel 25310 22222

SERRES
Serres Prefectural General Hospital,   tel 23210 94500

THESPROTIA
Filiates Prefectural General Hospital,   tel 26640 22203

THESSALONIKI
Agios Dimitrios Hospital,   tel 2310 203 121
AHEPA University Hospital,   tel 2310 993 310
Ipokratio Hospital,   tel 2310 837 921-9
Papanikolaou Hospital,   tel 2310 357 602
Yennimatas Hospital,   tel 2310 211 221-2

TRIKALA
Trikala Prefectural General Hospital,   tel 24310 45100

VIOTIA
Livadia Prefectural General Hospital,   tel 22610 20051

Thiva (Thebes) Prefectural
General Hospital,   tel 22620 24444
XANTHI
Xanthi Prefectural General Hospital,   tel 25410 47100

❏ TRANSPORT

ATHENS INTERNATIONAL AIRPORT ELEFTHERIOS VENIZELOS
tel 210 353 0000, website www.aia.gr
ATHENS-PIRAEUS TRAINS (ISAP),
67 Athinas, Athens tel 210 324 8311, website www.isap.gr
ATHENS-PIRAEUS TROLLEYS (ILPAP),
Ahaias & Kirkis sts, Kokkinos Milos, tel 210 258 3300
ATTIKO METRO
tel 210 519 4012, fax 210 519 4033,
website www.ametro.gr
HELLENIC RAILWAYS ORGANISATION (OSE), 1 Karolou,
Athens 104 37 tel 210 529 7002, website www.ose.gr
LONG-DISTANCE BUS SERVICE (KTEL)
tel 210 512 4910-11, website www.ktel.org
OLYMPIC AIRWAYS, 96 Syngrou, Athens tel 210 926 9111,
website www.olympic-airways.gr
**ORGANISATION OF ATHENS URBAN TRANSPORTATION
(OASA),** 15 Metsovou, Athens tel 210 883 6076,
website www.oasa.gr

TRANSPORT TIMETABLES (In Greek)
Timetables for:
Passenger Ships
Domestic Trains (departures)
International Trains (departures)
Intercity Buses (terminals)   1440
Public Transport Schedules   185

RADIO TAXI SERVICES (Athens)

ATHINA 1	tel 210 921 7942, 210 921 2800
APOLLON	tel 210 363 6508, 210 996 2262, 210 338 9055, 210 992 5200
APROODOS	tel 210 345 1200
ASTERAS	tel 210 614 4000, 210 971 1611, 210 492 2200, 210 614 3149
HELLAS NORTHEN SUBURBS	tel 80 111 37000, 210 801 4000
HELLAS SOUTHERN SUBURBS	tel 80 111 47000, 210 996 1420
HELLAS ATHENS PIRAEUS	tel 80 111 57000, 210 645 7000
HERMES	tel 210 411 5200, 210 411 5666,
EXPRESS	tel 210 993 4812, 210 994 3000
IKAROS	tel 210 515 2800
KIFISSIA	tel 210 808 4000, 210 623 3100/5
KOSMOS	tel 18300
PARTHENON	tel 210 532 3300, 210 532 2882
PIRAEUS 1	tel 210 418 2333, 80 111 36000
PROTOPORIA	tel 210 213 0400, 210 246 6633
RADIO TAXI EUROPE	tel 210 502 0357, 210 502 3583
RADIO TAXI GLYFADA	tel 210 960 5600

❏ MUSEUMS AND SITES

ACADEMY OF ATHENS, 28 Panepistimou
tel 210 360 0207, 210 360 0209, 210 364 3073

ACROPOLIS MUSEUM AND SITE, Dion Areopagitou St
tel 210 321 0219, 210 323 6665

ACROPOLIS STUDIES CENTRE, 2-4 Makriyanni
tel 210 923 9381

ANCIENT AGORA, 24 Adrianou, Thissio
tel 210 321 0185

ATHENS CITY MUSEUM, 7 Paparigopoulou, Klathmonos Sq,
Athens tel 210 324 6164, 210 323 0168

ATHENS UNIVERSITY HISTORICAL MUSEUM, 5 Tholou &
Klepsydras, Plaka tel 210 324 0861

BENAKI MUSEUM, 1 Koumbari & Vas Sofias, Athens
tel 210 367 1000

BYZANTINE MUSEUM, 22 Vas Sofias, Athens
tel 210 721 1027, 210 723 2178

CENTRE FOR FOLK ART AND TRADITION
6 Ang Hatzimihali, Plaka tel 210 324 3987

CENTRE FOR THE STUDY OF TRADITIONAL POTTERY
4-6 Melidoni, Psyrri tel 210 331 8491-6

CHILREN'S ART MUSEUM
9 Kondrou, Plaka tel 210 331 2621, 210 331 2750

CHILDREN'S MUSEUM
14 Kydathineon, Plaka tel 210 331 2995-6

CYCLADIC & ANCIENT GREEK ART MUSEUM
4 Neofytou Douka, Kolonaki tel 210 722 8321-3

DIONYSSUS THEATRE SITE
Dion Areopagitou St, Athens, tel 210 322 4625

DODECANESE HOUSE OF VASSILIS & IRINI MOSKOVIS
119 Dodonis, Sepolia tel 210 512 6611

DROSINI MUSEUM
Ag Theodoron & Kyriakou sts, Kifissia, tel 210 801 2642

ELEFTHERIOS VENIZELOS MUSEUM
Eleftherias Park, Vas Sofias Ave, Athens, tel 210 722 4238

EPIGRAPHICAL MUSEUM
Tositsa St, Athens tel 210 821 7637, 210 823 2950

FRISSIRAS MUSEUM OF CONTEMPORARY PAINTING
3-7 Monis Asteriou, Plaka tel 210 323 4678,
210 324 1297

GREEK HISTORICAL COSTUME MUSEUM
7 Dimokritou, Kolonaki tel 210 362 9513

GOULANDRIS NATURAL HISTORY MUSEUM
13 Levidou, Kifissia tel 210 801 5870

GOUNAROPOULOS MUSEUM
6 Gounaropoulou & Frigias, Ano Ilissia tel 210 777 7601,
210 748 7657

JEWISH MUSEUM OF GREECE
39 Nikis, Athens tel 210 322 5582

KANELLOPOULOS MUSEUM
Theorias & Panos sts, Plaka tel 210 321 2313

KATINA PAXINOU MUSEUM
20 Agiou Konstantinou & 52 Menandrou, Athens
tel 210 522 1420

KERAMIKOS MUSEUM
148 Ermou, Athens tel 210 346 3552

KESARIANI MONASTERY
Ethnikis Antistaseos Ave, Kesariani, tel 210 723 6619

LALAOUNIS JEWELLERY MUSEUM
4A Karyatidon & 12 Kallisperi, Acropolis, tel 210 922 1044

MARITIME (NAUTICAL) MUSEUM
Akti Themistokleous St, Piraeus, tel 210 451 6264, 210 428 6430

MELINA MERCOURI CULTURAL CENTRE
66 Iraklidon & Thessalonikis, Thissio, tel 210 345 2150,
210 341 4466

MUSEUM OF GREEK FOLK ART
17 Kydathineon, Plaka tel 210 322 9031

NATIONAL ARCHAEOLOGICAL MUSEUM
44 Patission, Athens tel 210 821 7717, 210 821 7724

NATIONAL ART GALLERY
AND ALEXANDROS SOUTZOS MUSEUM
60 Vas Sofias & Mihalakopoulou (close to the Hilton)
tel 210 723 5937-8, 210 723 5857

NATIONAL GARDENS BOTANICAL MUSEUM
Zappeio tel 210 721 5019

NATIONAL HISTORY MUSEUM
Stadiou & Kolokotroni sts, Athens, tel 210 323 7617

NATIONAL MUSEUM OF CONTEMPORARY ART
tel 210 924 2111-2

NATIONAL WAR MUSEUM
2 Rizari & Vas Sofias, Athens tel 210 724 4464

NUMISMATIC MUSEUM
12 Panepistimiou, Athens tel 210 364 3774

OLYMPIC ZEUS' TEMPLE
2 Vas Olgas & Amalias, Athens tel 210 922 6330

OTE MUSEUM
25 Proteos, Nea Kifissia tel 210 620 1899

PARLIAMENT
2 Vas Sofias, Athens tel 210 370 7000

PERANDINOS MUSEUM
14 Eforionos, Pangrati tel 210 751 3653

PHILATELIC (POSTAL) MUSEUM
2 Fokianou & 5 Panathinaikou Stadiou Sq, Athens tel 210 751 9066, 210 751 9042

PIRAEUS ARCHAEOLOGICAL MUSEUM
31 Harilaou Trikoupi, Piraeus tel 210 452 1598

POPULAR (FOLK) MUSICAL INSTRUMENTS MUSEUM
1-3 Diogenis, Aeridon Sq, Plaka tel 210 325 0198

RAILWAY/TRAIN MUSEUM
4 Siokou, Athens tel 210 512 6295

ROMAN FORUM SITE
Pelopida & Aeolou sts, Athens tel 210 324 5220

SPATHARION MUSEUM OF SHADOW THEATRE
Vas Sofias & Dimitriou Ralli sts, Kastalias Sq, Maroussi
tel 210 612 7245

THEATRICAL MUSEUM
50 Akadimias, Athens tel 210 362 9430

TOWER OF WINDS
Beginning of Aeolou St, Roman Agora, Plaka tel 210 324 5220

TSAROUHIS MUSEUM
28 Ploutarhou, Maroussi tel 210 806 2636

TSIDARAKI FOLK CERAMIC MUSEUM (OLD MOSQUE)
Monastiraki Sq, tel 210 324 2066

YANNIS AND ZOE SPYROPOULOS FOUNDATION
5 Phaedra, Ekali tel 210 813 4265, 210 813 3420

NEAR ATHENS

AEGINA MUSEUM AND KOLONA SITE, Kolona, Aegina
tel 22970 22248

CORINTH MUSEUM AND SITE, Ancient Corinth
tel 27410 31207

DELPHI MUSEUM AND SITE, Ancient Delphi
tel 22650 82312

ELEFSINA MUSEUM AND SITE, Ancient Elefsis
tel 210 554 6019

EPIDAVROS MUSEUM AND SITE, Ancient Epidavros
tel 27530 22009

MISTRA MUSEUM AND SITE, Mistra, Peloponnese
tel 27310 83377

MYCENAE SITE, Ancient Mycenae, Peloponnese
tel 27510 76585, 27510 76802

NAFPLIO MUSEUM, Nafplio, Peloponnese tel 27520 27502

NAFPLIO KOMBOLOI (PRAYER BEADS) MUSEUM
25 Staikopoulou, Nafplio 212 00, tel 27520 21618

OLYMPIA MUSEUM AND SITE
Olympia, Peloponnese tel 26240 22742, 26240 22517

OLYMPIA GAMES MUSEUM (HISTORICAL)
Olympia, Peloponnese tel 26240 29119,

SOUNIO ARCHAEOLOGICAL SITE (TEMPLE OF POSEIDON)
Sounio, Attica tel 22920 39363

VORRES MUSEUM OF CONTEMPORARY ART
4 Diadohou Konstantinou, Peania, Attica, tel 210 664 2520,
210 664 4771

MUSEUMS ON THE ISLANDS

CRETE

ARCHAEOLOGICAL MUSEUM OF AGIOS NIKOLAOS	tel 28410 24943
ARCHAEOLOGICAL MUSEUM OF HANIA,	tel 28210 90334
ARCHAEOLOGICAL MUSEUM OF IRAKLIO,	tel 2810 224630
ARCHAEOLOGICAL MUSEUM OF RETHYMNO,	tel 28310 54668

CYCLADES

ARCHAEOLOGICAL MUSEUM OF ANDROS,	tel 22820 23664
GOULANDRIS MUSEUM OF MODERN ART, Andros Hora,	tel 22820 22444,
Athens Office:	tel 210 725 2895
ARCHAEOLOGICAL MUSEUM OF DILOS	tel 22890 22259
ARCHAEOLOGICAL MUSEUM OF MILOS, Plaka	tel 22870 21620

ARCHAEOLOGICAL MUSEUM OF NAXOS, tel 22850 22725

ARCHAEOLOGICAL MUSEUM OF PAROS,
Parikia   tel 22840 21231

ARCHAEOLOGICAL MUSEUM OF SANTORINI,
Fira   tel 22860 22217

ARCHAEOLOGICAL MUSEUM OF SIFNOS,
Kastro   tel 22840 31022

ARCH'AEOLOGICAL MUSEUM OF SYROS,
Ermoupolis   tel 22810 88487

ARCHAEOLOGICAL MUSEUM OF TINOS,   tel 22830 29063

❏ THEATRES & HALLS

NATIONAL OPERA, 59 Akadimias, Athens, 210 361 1516

NATIONAL THEATRE, Ag Konstantinou &
Koumoundourou sts, Athens, 210 522 0585

MEGARON MOUSIKIS CONCERT HALL,
Vas Sofias & Kokkali sts, Athens, 210 728 2333,
website www.megaron.gr

MEGARON MOUSIKIS THESSALONIKI, 25th Martiou St
and Paralia tel 2310-895800

Irodion (Herod Atticus) Theatre, Dionyssiou Areopagitou St,
Athens: for events contact the Greek Festival box-office,
39 Panepistimiou St, tel 210 928 2900 or the Irodion Theatre
box-office, tel 210 323 2771

Lykavittos Theatre Lykavittos box-office at 210 722 7233

❏ ATTICA MUNICIPALITIES

ATHENS

ATHENS tel 210 331 2420/2, 210 527 7000;
fax 210 524 6943; web: www.cityofathens.gr;

email: webmaster@cityofathens.gr;

AEGALEO tel 210 531 5670/5, 210 531 5667/8; fax 210 531 5669; web: www.egaleo.gr; email: degaleo@asda.gr;

AGIA PARASKEVI tel 210 639 1511, 210 608 0224-4; fax 210 608 0183; web: www.agiaparaskevi.gr; email: dimarhos@agparaskevi.gr;

AGIA VARVARA tel 210 561 6709/569 0027; fax 210 540 2410 web: www.agiavarvara.gr; email:dab@asda.gr;

AGII ANARGYRI tel 210 261 6359, 210 261 6666; fax 210 261 1683; email: agiianargiri@asda.gr;

AGIOS DIMITRIOS tel 210 971 9111, 210 970 2500, 210 973 0132; fax 210 971 4303; web: www.dad.gr; email: dad-may@ars.net.gr;

ALIMOS tel 210 988 5717, 210 985 0009; fax 210 982 9249; web: www.alimos.gr; email: info@dimos-alimou.gr;

ARGYROUPOLI tel 210 991 8641, 210 991 8025; fax 210 992 7024; web: www.argyroupoli.gr; email: dimarhos@argyroupoli.gr;

DAFNI tel 210 971 1451, 210 971 1210; fax 210 975 0614;

EKALI tel 210 813 1286, fax 210 813 7660

ELLINIKO tel 210 961 8283, 210 961 6541; fax 210 963 3417; web: www.dimosellinikou.gr; email: contact@dimosellinikou.gr;

FILOTHEI tel 210 681 2574, 210 681 2171; fax 210 684 8702; web: www.filothei.gr;

GALATSI tel 210 291 6106, 210 292 1512; fax 210 291 8120; web: galatsi.gr;

email: galatis@otenet.gr;

GLYFADA tel 210 891 2300, 210 698 0590/1;
fax 210 894 7719; web: dimotologio@glyfada.gr;

HAIDARI tel 210 581 1621, 210 532 582 2040;
fax 210 581 9841;dhdim@otenet.gr;

HALANDRI tel 210 680 0000, 210 681 1828;
fax 210 684 3009; web: www.halandri.gr;
email: webmaster@halandri.gr;

HOLARGOS tel 210 652 1245, 210 651 2171;
fax 210 651 3840; web: www.mum-cholargos.gr;
email: holargos@onteragora.gr

ILION (NEA LIOSSIA) tel 210 261 8642, 210 261 5964;
fax 210 261 0300; web: www.ilion.gr;
email ilion@ilion.gr;

ILIOUPOLI tel 210 997 0000; fax 210 992 3340;
web: www.cityofilioupolis.gr; email: zogr100@otenet.gr;

IRAKLIO tel 210 277 7511-15, 210 277 1949;
fax 210 277 7516; web: www.iraklio.gr;
email: dimaraklio@iraklio.gr;

KALLITHEA tel 210 957 3150-3, 210 957 3350-9;
fax 210 956 0171; email: kalithea@otenet.gr;

KAMATERO tel 210 238 4500-4, 210 231 6018;
fax 210 231 6017; email: d.kama@tee.gr

KESSARIANI tel 210 729 2601-8; fax 210 729 2621;
web: www.kessariani.gr; email: dkaisar@hol.gr;

KIFISSIA tel 210 628 9000; fax 210 808 7090;
web: www.kifissia.gr; email: dkifisia@otenet.gr

LYKOVRISSI tel 210 281 9171, 210 282 7374;
fax 210 281 9449; web: www.likovrisi.gr;
email: likovrisi@likovrisi.gr;

MAROUSSI tel 210 876 0000, 210 876 0302
fax 210 876 0500, web: www.maroussi2004.gr
email: amaroussion@maroussi2004.gr
MELISSIA tel 210 803 5081-5; fax 210 804 0438;
METAMORFOSSI tel 210 283 2691, 210 281 8808;
fax 210 281 3207; web: www.metamorfossi.gr;
MOSCHATO tel 210 941 2853, 210 941 6669;
fax 210 941 6154;
NEA ERYTHREA tel 210 800 0222, 210 1275;
fax 210 800 0259; web: www.dne.gov.gr;
NEA HALKIDONA tel 210 251 1470, 210 251 6405;
fax 210 252 6580; email: neahalki@otenet.gr;
NEA IONIA tel 210 279 0115,210 279 0872;
fax 210 279 2500; web: www.dimonseasionias.gr;
NEA PHILADELPHIA tel 210 251 0100, 210 258 4400-7;
fax 210 252 4512; web: www.filadelfeia-dimos.gr;
email: nfcc@ath.forthnet.gr
NEO PSYCHIKO tel 210 671 2558, 210 671 7211;
fax 210 672 2859; web: www.cityofnewpsychico.gr;
email: mayor@cityofnewpsychico.gr;
NEA SMYRNI tel 210 937 6700, 210 937 6851;
fax 210 937 6846; web: www.neasmyrni.net.gr;
PALEO FALIRO tel 210 981 5005, 210 981 5805;
fax 210 983 3736;
PAPAGOU tel 210 654 0700-4; fax 210 652 8472;
web: www.dimos-papagou.gr;
email: papagos@interagora.gr;
PEFKI tel 210 612 5425, 210 806 8388, 210 612 5465
fax 210 614 1356; web: www.dimospefkis.gr;
PERISTERI tel 210 574 0201-10, 210 571 1351;
fax 210 571 1492;
PETROUPOLI tel 210 506 5400, 210 505 5390

fax 210 501 9477; email: dimoto@petroupoli.gr;
PSYCHIKO tel 210 672 6081-5, 210 672 2334;
fax 210 672 2934; web: www.psychiko.gr;
TAVROS tel 210 345 5378, 210 346 2101;
fax 210 346 1241;
web: ww.dimostavrou.gr; email: tayros@mail.otenet.gr;
VRYLISSIA tel 210 682 3785, 210 681 2672
fax 210 681 5686 email: dimarhos@otenet.gr
VYRONAS tel 210 765 2411, 210 766 1879
fax 210 766 9596
YMITTOS tel 210 762 4804, 210 762 5700
fax 210 762 3859;
ZOGRAFOU tel 210 749 0101/30; 210 777 5950;
fax 210-779 5545

LOCAL GOVERNMENT COUNCILS

NEA PENDELI tel 210 804 0523, 210 804 3104
fax 210 804 2302
PENDELI tel 210 804 1449, fax 210 804 1168

EAST ATTICA

AGIOS STEFANOS tel 210-814 0030, 210 814 2474,
210 621 9015, fax 210-814 1421
AHARNON tel 210 241 5300-1, fax 210 246 4022
ARTEMIS (LOUTSA) tel 22940-81800-3, fax 22940-45560
AVLONA tel 22950-41264, 22950-41811,
22950-41178, 22950-42212 fax 22950-41931
GLYKA NERA tel 210 665 9106, 210 665 9823,
fax 210 665 9822
KALIVIA THORIKOU tel 22990 48332, 22990-48289,
22990-48665, fax 22990- 48289,
email: dkalivia@otenet.gr
KERATEA tel 22990 69240, 22990 68340,
fax 22990 67900

KOROPI tel 210 662 8405, 210 662 6559,
210 662 3628, fax 210 662 4963
LAVRIO tel 22920 25225, 22920 25060,
22920 25150 fax 22920 22413
MARATHON tel 22940 66240, 22940 66281,
fax 22940 66282
MARKOPOULO MESOGIA tel 22990 20000,
22990 20121, fax 22990 24003,
web: www.markopoulo.gr
email: webmaster@markopoulo.gr
NEA MAKRI tel 22940 91272, 22940 91230,
fax 22940 94415 email: Neamakri@ath.forthnet.gr
PALLINI tel 210 666 6059, 210 666 8612
fax 210 666 7870
PEANIA tel 210 664 2344, 210 664 2580,
210 664 6130, fax 210 664 6188
RAFINA tel 22940 23681, 22940 24444, 22940 28560,
fax 22940 23481, web: www.arafin.gr
email: Dhmosraf@arafin.gr
SPATA tel 210 663 2200, 210 663 2222,
fax 210 6633 311, web: www.spata.gr
VARI tel 210 8972160, 210 8971665 fax 210 8970741;
web: www.vari.gr; email: info@vari.gr;

VOULA tel 210 8958228, 210 8953851-4,
fax 210 895 9990; web: www.dimosvoulas.gr;

VOULIAGMENI tel 210 8960156, 210 896 0196;
fax 210 896 3627;

YERAKAS tel 210 661 1853, 210 661 1854,
fax 210 661 2965;

LOCAL GOVERNMENT COUNCILS
AFIDNE tel 22950 22883, fax 22950 22227
ANAVYSSOS tel 22910 36212, 22910 41220/2/3

fax 22910 41219

ANIXI tel 210 621 6127, fax 210 814 2421

ANTHOUSA tel 210 603 1446, 210 666 7764, fax 210 603 1069

DIONYSSOS tel 210 815 0792, 210 621 1162, fax 210 815 0821

DROSIA tel/fax 210 813 1332

GRAMMATIKO tel 22940 61144, fax 22940 61147

KALAMOS tel 22950 62118, fax 22950 29480

KAPANDRITI tel 22950 52418, fax 22950 53107

KOUVARA tel 22990 67940, fax 22990 68743

KRYONERI tel 210 816 1354, 210 816 1693, fax 210 816 1684, web: www.kryoneri.gr email: Koinotita@kryoneri.gr

MALAKASSA tel 22950 98296, fax 22950 98596

MARKOPOULOS OROPOU tel 22950 32429, 22950 30358, fax 22950 32376

OROPION tel 22950 32435, fax 22950 30640

PALEA FOKEA tel 22910 38721, fax 22910 36260

PIKERMI tel 210 603 9550, fax 210 603 9245

POLYDENDRI tel 22950 52498, 22950 54217, fax 22950 53106

RODOPOLEOS tel 210 621 0804-5, fax 210 621 0804

SARONIDA tel 22910 54444, fax 22910 53784

SIKAMINOU tel 22950 71792, fax 22950 71754

STAMATA tel 210 621 8051, fax 210 621 8111

THRAKOMAKEDONES tel 210 243 2300, 210 243 1668, fax 210 243 3256

VARNAVAS tel 22950 97249, fax 22950 97412

WEST ATTICA

ANO LIOSSIA tel 210 247 4845-9, 210 247 4377, fax 210 247 4401, web: www.liosia.gr email: Liosia@liosia.gr

ASPROPYRGOS tel 210 557 2698, 210 557 3216, 210 557 1805, fax 210 557 2276, web: www.cityofaspropyrgos.gr email: dimos@cityofaspropyrgos.gr

ELEFSINA tel 210 553 7302-4, 210 553 7100, fax 210 553 7254 web: www.elefsina.gr email: gd@elefsina.gr, elefsina@otenet.gr

ERYTHRES tel 22630 62212, 22630 62268, fax 22630 63340

FYLI tel 210 241 1702, 210 241 1444, fax 210 241 1011, web: www.dimosfylis.gr email: info@dimosfylis.gr, dimosfylis@dimosfylis.gr

MANDRA tel 210 555 5745, 210 555 5066, fax 210 555 5880

MEGARA tel 22960 81007, 22960 81841, fax 22960 81632, 22960 81841, web: www.megara.gr email: dhmegara@otenet.gr

NEA PERAMOS tel 22960 33203, 22960 32609, 22960 32550, fax 22960 33203

VILLIA tel 22630 22515, 22630 22630, 22630 22993, fax 22630 22204

ZEFYRI tel 210 231 5260, 210 231 9066, 210 231 9026, fax 210 231 9026

LOCAL GOVERNMENT COUNCILS

INOI tel 22630 51396, fax 22630 51271

MAGOULA tel 210 555 5443, fax 210 555 7816

PIRAEUS

AEGINA tel 22970 22409, 22970 22220, fax 22970 25099, web: www.aegina.gr email:aegina@hellasnet.gr

AGIOS IOANIS RENDI, tel 210 483 8810, 210 481 3680, 210 482 5700, fax 210 481 5676, web: www.cityofrentis.gr email: info@cityofrentis.gr

AMBELAKIA tel 210 467 1970, fax 210 467 1713, web: http:ampelakia.gr email: dimamp+08@otenet.gr

DRAPETSONA, tel 210 462 0902, 210 462 8529, fax 210 462 0968

HYDRA tel 22980 52210, 22980 53003, fax 22980 53482, web: www.hydra.gr

KERATSINI, tel 210 461 2712, 210 461 7887, fax 210 461 5387, 210 461 2361, web: www.keratsinipeople.gr

KORYDALLOS tel 210 499 0400, 210 499 0702-3, 210 494 2003, fax 210 499 0404, web:www.korydallos.gr email: korydal1@otenet.gr, Korydal@otenet.gr

METHANA tel 22980 92324, 22980 92269, fax 22980 92437, email: methana@otenet.gr

NIKEA tel 210 427 8100, 210 427 8160, fax 210 427 8162, email:Info@polisnikaia.gr

PERAMA, tel 210 441 1551, 210 441 1565, 210 441 0993, 210 441 5903, fax 210 402 1373, web: www.dperama.gr email: Perama@ath.forthnet.gr

PIRAEUS, tel 210 419 4000, 210 419 4281-8, fax 210 419 4290

POROS, tel 22980 22250, 22980 22220, 22980 23089, fax 22980 25353

SALAMINA, tel 210 464 6100, 210 464 6000-10,
210 464 6100, fax 210 464 6190,
web: www.salamina.gr email:Salamina@panafonet.gr

SPETSES, tel 22980 72225, 22980 72588,
22980 74509, fax 22980 73366

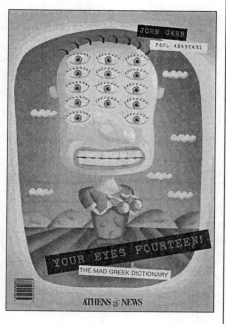